VAMP

VAMP

THE RISE AND FALL OF THEDA BARA

BY EVE GOLDEN

INTRODUCTION BY ROBERT S. BIRCHARD

EMPRISE PUBLISHING, INC.
VESTAL, NEW YORK

To My Sister, Debbi Golden

A Bit of a Vamp in Her Own Right

Front cover illustration: Publicity still originally taken by Mishkin for *Sin* (1915). *Photo: The Everett Collection.*

Illustration facing title page: *Photo: Jerry Ohlinger.*

Cover design: Don Bell

ISBN 1-887322-00-0 cloth binding
ISBN 1-879511-32-0 trade paperback
Library of Congress Catalog Card Number 95-83363

First Printing January 1996, cloth
Second Printing April 1998, trade paper
Printed in the USA.

Published by
Emprise Publishing, Inc.
4700 Marshall Drive West
Vestal, New York 13850

Table of Contents

Photo: Gene Andrewski.

Acknowledgements

I'd like to thank the following people and institutions for assisting in the research for this book and helping to make the writing move along smoothly:

David Blazak; Robert S. Birchard; Raymond Brabin; Christian Brandan; the late Alan Brock; Kevin Brownlow, David Gill, and Patrick Stanbury (Photoplay Productions); Margaret Byrne (American Film Institute); Catherine Childs; The Cincinnati Historical Society; the late Randye Cohen; Ned Comstock (University of Southern California); Olivia de Havilland; Victoria Demchick; Glen Distefano; Allen Ellenberger; The Fort Lee Public Library; the late Lillian Gish; Larry Givens; Lester Gottlieb; Keith Greene; Jack Hardy (Grapevine Video); Bob King (*Classic Images*); Manuel Lado; Dana Lauren; Dr. John F. Ledlie; Srs. Mary Magdalene, Margaret Mary and Kathleen Duffy (Marycrest Manor); Ronald Magliozzi (Museum of Modern Art, NY); Randal Malone; Grange McKinney; Arleen Moss (New York Public Library, Paper Prints Division); Anita Page; Michael Powazinik; Debbie Ruggles; Mark Sachleblen; Joyce Serkin (Walnut Hills High School); Charles Weissburd (Los Angeles County Clerk).

A biography without photos is like a cake without icing. Thanks to the following people and institutions for the photos in this book:

Gene Andrewski, Michael Ankerich, Arbe Bareis (Safka and Bareis), Robert S. Birchard, Lisa Bulger, Chester Clarke, Joseph P.

Vamp: The Rise and Fall of Theda Bara

Eckhardt, Kevin Grace, Ron Harvey and Mikko Macchione (The Everett Collection), Bruce Hershenson, Paula Klaw (Movie Star News), Ronald Magliozzi (Museum of Modern Art, NY), Albert Manski, Joe Martinez (The Motion Picture and Television Photo Archive), The New York Public Library at Lincoln Center, Eric Rachlis (Archive Photos), David J. Skal, Mary Anne Styburski, Diva Velez (Jerry Ohlinger's Movie Material Store), The Wisconsin Center for Film and Theater Research.

Introduction

What is one to make of Theda Bara?

Today, the actress is known largely as an image in still photographs — slightly ridiculous to our jaded eyes, and yet strangely compelling. She made forty-two films, but barring some unlikely miracle we will never experience what it was that made her one of the movies' first great stars. Bara's surviving films are not representative of what audiences and critics considered her best work.

Her life story is no more accessible. Theda Bara was a star in an age when fact and fancy about theatrical people were blended and blurred by publicist and press as a matter of course. By the time historians took an interest, the trail was cold. Theda Bara and her most frequent collaborators were no longer here to separate incident from invention.

For these reasons, I think, no one has attempted before now to write a book-length examination of her career. Yet this pop icon of a bygone day created a persona so potent that it still reverberates in our collective consciousness. Eve Golden is to be commended for taking on the challenge of evoking Theda Bara's life and work.

Superficially at least, the most interesting fact about "Theda Bara" is that she was not Theda Bara at all. Her off-screen personality was invented by imaginative flacks to suit her screen reflection. However, Bara was not alone in living a fabricated public role. Theatre and movies transformed Iowa-born William Grant Blandin into the fiery Corsican "Romaine Fielding." Serial star "Grace Cunard" was touted as a child of Paris, but in reality she was Harriet Mildred Jeffries from Columbus, Ohio. Mae Smith cultivated some distant Spanish ancestors and took "Marin Sais" as her professional name. "Princess Mona Darkfeather" was promoted as a full-blooded Seminole Indian even though her family knew her as Josephine M. Workman. The faux Russian tragédienne "Olga Petrova" sometimes dropped her heavily accented speech and reverted to the King's English she learned as Muriel Harding. Even "Mary Pickford" was born plain Gladys Smith. It was more than an exotic pseudo biography that made Theda Bara unique. The forgotten news that author Golden has uncovered offers surprising revelations about the legend and erases many previously held notions about Theda Bara and the people in the dark who idolized her.

On and off camera Theda Bara was more than the "rag, a bone, and a hank of hair" that personified the female predator imagined by Rudyard Kipling in his poem, "The Vampire." She transcended the "Kiss me, My Fool" dialogue titles that helped popularize the evil villainess of Porter Emerson Brown's *A Fool There Was* as the "Vamp" — a desired fantasy role-model for women, and a fantasy woman to be desired by men. As Golden points out, Bara's range was far wider than the stereotyped image that remains in our mind's eye.

That she became trapped in her screen image is a matter of record. When the vogue of the vamp evaporated shortly after the finish of "the war to end all wars," for all intents and purposes Theda Bara vanished from the screen. But even here there is more to the story than has been told previously.

After reading Golden's account, it seems to me that Theda Bara performed a remarkable balancing act by being true to herself and yet never playing false with her popular image. While she laughed at her reputation as "the wickedest woman on the screen," she ultimately had no desire to break the spell she had cast.

Oh, how I wish I could see Theda Bara in *Cleopatra*! But I wonder if the film itself could ever match my expectations? As

Golden recreates the opening scene of *Cleopatra* in words, the intense black-rimmed eyes of Theda Bara rivet me to my imaginary theatre chair, and again work their magic — and I think that it would indeed!

If we must settle for words at this late date, then I am thrilled to have Eve Golden's heartfelt account of Theda Bara's remarkable life. Short of discovering a means of traveling through time, it is as close as we are ever likely to get to meeting the screen's great Vamp!

Robert S. Birchard
Los Angeles, California
May 20, 1995
Film historian Birchard is the author of a book on another Fox star,
King Cowboy: Tom Mix and the Movies

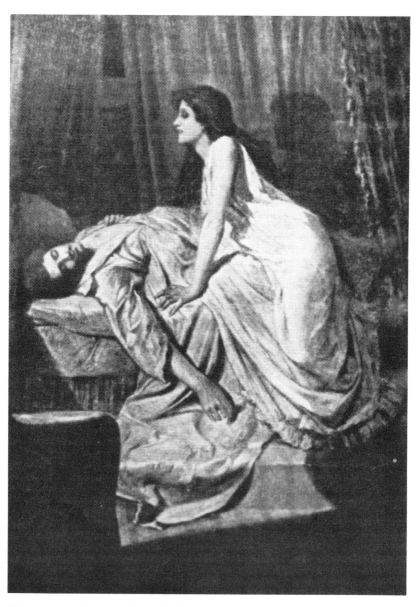

The painting that started it all: Philip Burne-Jones' *The Vampire*, exhibited in 1897 in London. The only explanation of the painting in the exhibition catalogue was the poem written by his cousin, Rudyard Kipling. The woman in the painting is identified as Mrs. Patrick Campbell, well-known actress. Theda Bara met her several decades later (see page 228). *Photo: David J. Skal.*

The Vampire

A Fool there was and he made his prayer —
(Even as you and I.)
To a rag and a bone and a hank of hair —
(We called her the woman who did not care)
But the fool he called her his lady fair —
(Even as you and I.)

Oh, the years we waste and the tears we waste —
And the work of our head and hand
Belong to the woman who did not know —
(And now we know that she never could know)
And did not understand.

A Fool there was and his goods he spent —
(Even as you and I.)
Valor and faith and sure intent —
(And it wasn't the least what the lady meant)
But a fool must follow his natural bent
(Even as you and I.)

Oh, the toil we lost and the spoil we lost —
And the excellent things we planned
Belong to the woman who didn't know why —
(And now we know she never knew why)
And did not understand.

The Fool was stripped to his foolish hide —
(Even as you and I.)
Which she might have seen when she threw him aside —
(But it isn't on record the lady tried)
So some of him lived but the most of him died —
(Even as you and I.)

But it isn't the shame, and it isn't the blame
That sting like a white hot brand —
It's coming to know that she never knew why —
(Seeing at last that she never knew why)
And could never understand.

Rudyard Kipling, 1897

Prologue

The Chicago hotel room was draped in Egyptian trimmings, sprayed with perfume, and bedecked in lilies and roses; deep velvet curtains were drawn and the room was stifling. Dozens of reporters had been invited by Fox Studios to meet the exotic foreign actress starring in their upcoming film, *A Fool There Was.*

Before the star herself was introduced, the ladies and gentlemen of the press wolfed down free food and drink and took notes while Fox's public relations men, Al Selig and John Goldfrap, provided background information on the actress. As famous as she may be in Paris, they smiled, Theda Bara was still fairly unknown in the U. S.

She was born in the shadow of the pyramids, Selig and Goldfrap related, the pampered only child of a French actress, Theda de Lyse, and an Italian sculptor, Guiseppe Bara. The adventurous de Lyse had been touring Egypt when she encountered Bara, lost in the desert sands. "His paints, his canvases, even his treasured trinkets had been thrown away in the delirium of one who is staring grim death in the face." The beautiful French actress saved his life, of course, and "it was the beginning of one of the world's sweetest romances."

In due time, little Theda was born to the dashing couple, who made their home in a huge tent not far from the Sphinx. "The oasis, our little home for years, was to us like the Garden of Eden," the little girl later sighed nostalgically. "My mother taught me the languages, expression, and the art of pantomime. On the other hand, my father taught me how to paint, and the beauty and combination of colors. And through the instruction of both I learned the symphony of the soul."

Soon little Theda moved to Paris with her parents. "To me, raised in the quiet of Egypt, it was wonderful," Selig and Goldfrap quoted the still-hidden star. Taking after her mother, she acted in Jane Hading's company, then the Grand Guignol, "because of her serpentine figure and flashing black eyes of the desert." Then came the Gymnase, the Théâtre Antoine ("the French capital's theatre of thrills"), where she had "a following second to none in Paris." Finally, she was discovered by film director Frank Powell. With the onset of war in 1914, Powell and the exotic actress escaped to the safety of America.

After the reporters were up to date on the amazing history of Theda Bara, the drawing room curtains parted dramatically to reveal The Serpent of the Nile herself: the pale-skinned, black-haired actress reclined languidly on a chaise draped with tiger skins; she was dressed in velvet and veils in the sweltering heat. Selig and Goldfrap excused the atmosphere, explaining that the Arabian star was not accustomed to the frigid January air of Chicago.

Theda took no questions, but her statements sounded suspiciously well tuned for a recent immigrant. "I am delighted to have this opportunity of displaying my work to American spectators," she said with "a Gallic shrug," "and I hope I have succeeded in depicting the complex emotions of this woman as vividly as they have appealed to me." The character she played in her new film, Theda purred, possessed a heart that was "a charnel house of men's dead hopes and withered ambitions . . . This vampire of mine possesses only one good or decent quality, her courage. Some night when she faces old age and her mirror shows her wrinkles, she will [kill herself]. Gas or poison, I should think. But nothing that would disfigure her."

Prologue

After the press conference, the reporters were ushered out —
all except one. Young Louella Parsons — not yet a famous Hollywood gossip columnist — witnessed the Arabian star ripping her
veils and coat off, staggering to the window, throwing it open, and
gasping in perfect mid-American, "Give me air!"

THEDA BARA

COPYRIGHT. C.M-410 B.
CINEMA STARS.

FOX PICTURE STAR.

LILYWHITE LTD
ALL BRITISH PHOTO PRINTERS

Photo: Lisa Bulger.

Chapter 1

The Thread of Destiny

In the mid-1930's, a group of well-dressed middle-aged women met at a chic Hollywood restaurant for luncheon. Major stars flitted through the room, eating, chatting, signing autographs and trying to avoid the stares of tourists. Gloria Swanson, Jean Harlow, Joan Bennett glittered and laughed self-consciously. Newspaper columnist Louis Sobol was there too, looking for fodder for his gossip column.

He spotted the group of ladies off to one side, looking for all the world, he wrote, like "Dubuque housewives on a tour." Then he looked a little closer at one of them: a pretty, slightly buxom woman in her forties, with rich black hair. It was her "large slumberous eyes" that attracted Sobol's notice. With some shock he realized he was looking at Theda Bara, who had been one of the screen's greatest stars some fifteen years earlier.

Still relatively young and attractive, Bara sat otherwise unnoticed through lunch. She paid the bill and went back to her wealthy director husband and comfortable Beverly Hills home, leaving Sobol to write a stunned column the next day. To hear him tell it, he might have encountered Madame DuBarry, Cleopatra, or some other figure of ancient history, rather than a woman still young enough to be on-screen herself. Theda Bara, in little over a decade, had become a musty historical figure with little or no connection to modern-day life. Today, she is the least accessible of silent stars, most of her films missing, and the few that exist showing her off poorly.

Amazingly, no full-length biography has ever been written of Theda Bara, though all books on cinema admit her importance in film history. Over the past few decades, biographies or autobiographies of nearly every other important figure of the silent screen have appeared, but nothing on Theda Bara.

Perhaps the lack of scandal in her life has discouraged writers and publishers: Theda Bara never had a substance abuse problem and her only marriage was a happy one. She lived to a decent old age and died wealthy. Unlike Joan Crawford, Loretta Young, Bette Davis, and Marlene Dietrich, Theda never had a child to vilify her in print. The fact that her films are largely unavailable also makes her a slippery subject for a book. The ludicrous childhood stories and faked interviews distributed by her film studio make the facts of her life tough to pin down.

In 1918, Theda Bara was one of the three top stars in movies, ranking behind only Mary Pickford and Charlie Chaplin. She single-handedly saved Fox Studios. And — even in her most ludicrous vamp films — she was idolized by millions of fans and praised by hard-nosed film critics. But by the time talking pictures became popular, she was all but forgotten.

How did such a star's enormous reputation plummet so quickly in the public's mind? For one thing, Theda Bara belongs entirely to the silent era. Unlike Pickford, Douglas Fairbanks, Chaplin, Buster Keaton, Harold Lloyd, Norma Talmadge, the Gish sisters, and other contemporaries, she never once spoke on-screen. She did not have the career-enhancing fate of an early death which gave Rudolph Valentino, Marilyn Monroe, and James Dean such morbid cachet. She never distinguished herself on Broadway, though not for lack of trying.

Theda Bara also did not live long enough to be re-discovered. Lillian Gish, Blanche Sweet, Gloria Swanson and other stars eventually found themselves to be historical icons, interviewed and fawned over by those too young to remember the silent screen. But when Theda died in 1955, silent movies were only a faintly embarrassing memory, more to be laughed at than studied. Theda's nitrate films were crumbling to dust or going up in flames through the 1940's and 1950's, but no one cared much, not even Theda herself.

The only thing keeping her from vanishing completely were those eyes that arrested Louis Sobol. Even today, photos of Theda — with her enormous kohl-rimmed eyes, severe dark lips and bizarre costumes — show up in posters, ads and greeting cards.

But even now, when silent films are studied in schools, lionized in museums and written about in book after book, people do not quite know what to make of Theda Bara. She is far too important to ignore and is always mentioned as the first sex symbol, the first publicity-created star, the first "vamp." But many writers still dismiss her as the untalented invention of some publicity men. Only a few suggest that — just possibly — she was a decent actress, trapped in scores of bad films.

When I started this book, I had seen Theda in *A Fool There Was, The Unchastened Woman* and *Madame Mystery*, and was not overly impressed with her talent. But when I began to dig deeper, to read what her peers and contemporary newspaper critics had to say, I realized that to underrate Theda Bara was a serious mistake and a misrepresentation of film history.

Theda Bara was, of course, the film's first sex symbol and first publicity-created star. But she was more than that. A surprising number of contemporary film reviewers felt that Theda was one of the great talents of her time, and fan magazines ran poll after poll proving her great popularity. Additionally, Theda's career took place at a pivotal time in film history. When she started her career in late 1914, American films were still fairly crude and amateurish; most were made on the East Coast. By the time she retired in late 1919, Hollywood was well on its way to becoming the world's film capital, and the Golden Age of the movies had begun. Theda was an integral part of this development.

Vamp: The Rise and Fall of Theda Bara

I also found Theda Bara to be an engaging and unusual person, quite unusual for a sex symbol: I don't believe Theda set foot inside a nightclub until her retirement. From a solemn and self-important teenager, she grew into a humorous and intelligent woman with a great sense of perspective on herself and her career.

Until a few years ago, many silent stars were still with us to put forth their own claims to history, to give their own interviews. Today, sadly, the field is evening out: nearly everyone who appeared in or worked in the earlier silent films is gone. Only ten years ago, many people in their eighties and nineties shared brilliant first-hand memories of the era with us; now few are left. In another few years the silent film era — just the day before yesterday, really — will have slipped away irretrievably into the past.

It's time for a reappraisal of Theda Bara.

Chapter 2

The Lure of Ambition

The facts of Theda Bara's childhood were so re-shuffled and re-imagined by her studio that they are difficult to uncover even today. Even more difficult to ascertain is the background of her parents. We know much more about the "Italian artist" and "French actress" invented by Fox's publicity department than we do about Bernard Goodman and Pauline Louise Françoise deCoppet.

Bernard Goodman was an Americanized name, probably bestowed on its owner upon his arrival in this country, decades before Ellis Island began greeting immigrants. He was born in "Poland, Russia" (according to his citizenship papers) in 1853 and came to New York in 1871. One or two writers have guessed that he may have been born in Chorzow, not far from Krakow. By 1882, Goodman had settled in Cincinnati, found work as a fabric cutter, and had become a U.S. citizen, officially renouncing allegiance to The Emperor of Russia.

Theda's mother was born in Switzerland in 1861; she was still a child when her French father, François Baranger, and her German mother, Regine deCoppet Baranger, died. By her own melodramatic account, Pauline and her sister were entrusted to their uncle ("court surgeon to the first Emperor") who soon relocated to America. Pauline, too, made her way to Ohio. By 1878 Pauline was working as a saleslady; she eventually became a wigmaker (her rather alarming entry in the local address book read, "DeCoppet, P. L. human hair"). By 1880 she was the co-owner of Dunkelmeyer & DeCoppet wigmakers.

Bernard and Pauline married in 1882. Bernard was employed

as foreman cutter in a tailor shop. He worked his way up to become a designer, and finally (in 1899) co-owner of Ochs, Weihl & Goodman, tailors. The Goodmans moved to an apartment at Eighth and Elm. And moved. And moved. The Goodman family spent much time packing and unpacking, as they relocated to various addresses in the Cincinnati area: Broadway, Taft, then progressively larger houses on Church Avenue in Walnut Hills (1887), and in Mt. Auburn (1889). Even when the family settled in the Cincinnati suburb of Avondale, they couldn't keep still, moving to Mitchell Avenue (1890), Harvey Avenue (1891), 3561 Rosedale Place (1896) and 823 Hutchins Avenue (1899).

The Goodmans' first child, Theodosia (nicknamed "Theda," or "Teddy") was born on July 29, 1885, followed by Marque ("Buddy"), in 1888. In 1897, when Theda was twelve, the last addition to the Goodman family was born: Esther ("Lori"). The three children got along very well, especially the two girls. Theda (named for Aaron Burr's ill-fated daughter) was a plump, dark-haired girl and her baby sister Lori a delicate blonde. Despite their life-long, close friendship, there may have been a little envy on Theda's part. Theda later insisted that she herself had been a thin, frail blonde child, and that every night she prayed to grow up as a tall, dark lady. She did indeed grow up to be that lady, but childhood photos reveal her to be a sullen butterball next to angelic little Lori.

The Goodmans didn't want for anything, and Theda's childhood appears to have been idyllic. Avondale was a wonderful neighborhood to grow up in. In the 1830's, wealthy Cincinnati businessmen built luxurious homes there and it became a thriving community by the 1870's. Stores, schools and plush residential areas sprung up. The town was marked by large Victorian homes of stone and gingerbread woodwork, parks, well-kept lawns, and imposing public buildings like Avon Hall.

The house owned by the Goodmans on Hutchins Avenue was

Left: Theodosia Goodman, ca. 1886. *Right:* Theodosia showing off her nautical poses, ca. 1890. *Photos: Motion Picture Classic Magazine, Chester Clarke.*

823 Hutchins Avenue, where Theda lived with her family from 1899 until she left for New York in 1905. *1995 photo by Kevin Grace.*

certainly comfortable, if hardly a mansion. An envious neighbor later described it as having "a carriage stone in front of their house to step down on from their carriage. It said Goodman on it. We were impressed by that." Equally impressive was the fact that the Goodmans employed two native-born servant girls. It was general practice to hire innocent immigrants "right off the boat," but the maids employed by the Goodmans as of the 1900 census are listed as Anna Tusinig, born in Kentucky, and Ida Deyberth, an Ohio native.

Being Jewish, the Goodmans had chosen a favorable place to live. Avondale had a strong, close-knit Jewish population, mostly well-to-do immigrants from Germany and Poland. Theda was Bat Mitzvahed in 1898 by Rabbi David Philipson at the Mound Street Temple and, though never very religious, was always proud of her heritage. Jewish religious and charitable groups abounded in Cincinnati: the Adath Israel Congregation was formed in 1846, Gemilath Chesed in 1891, Anshe Poland in 1896 and the Young Women's Improvement Club in 1897.

Theda's home state was also somewhat of a political hotbed, being the birthplace of the Women's Christian Temperance Union, the Populist and Prohibition Parties, and Presidents Cleveland and McKinley. Ohio also granted women the right to vote in 1894, well ahead of the United States government.

But Avondale was, basically, a small town in the heyday of small towns. Theda's childhood consisted of school, occasional trips, county fairs, playing with her siblings and — mostly — reading. Theda found her best friends in books, and for the rest of her life, was never really happy unless she had one book on her lap and another two at the ready. Lori and Marque eagerly went off to the woods behind the Goodmans' Rosedale Place home for cook-outs, while Theda sneaked upstairs to read. Unlike most Victorian girls, she never even learned to sew or embroider, as she couldn't be pried away from her books long enough.

2 / The Lure of Ambition

But she could also be a strong-minded and mischievous child. Her parents were rather relieved when books began taking up her time, as pre-school Theda was quite a handful. She loved playing dress-up, frequently purloining her mother's feathered hats and sweeping gowns. Once, a frustrated Pauline locked Theda in a closet as punishment. "She was so quiet I became frightened and opened the door," Pauline wrote years later, "and there she was dressing up in my clothes, trying on my hats and having a perfectly wonderful time. Such punishment was obviously futile."

Little Theda ran away from home at every opportunity and, according to her mother, "showed a positive genius in ways and means of escaping our vigilance. We had the locks in the entrance doors place high above her tiny reach and yet she disappeared as if by magic." Once she escaped wearing her mother's best gown and hat, trailing them down the street with a frantic Pauline in pursuit. Much to her mother's shock, "we afterwards discovered she had hammered a small hole in the screen door, just large enough to crawl through." Screen doors had only been introduced in the 1880's, so it was an expensive luxury that Theda had destroyed.

Finally the Goodmans had to build an improvised cage in the back yard for their wayward daughter. "I shall never forget the intense interest with which she watched the construction of that fence," said Pauline, "and the screams and kicks when she discovered she was trapped."

Her flair for the dramatic often led Theda into trouble. When she was about six, her neighborhood was plagued by a peculiarly benign child molester, who would sneak up behind little girls and snip off their hair. Theda found this fascinating, and was more and more annoyed as the days went by and she — closely watched by the Goodmans' gardener, Ike Williams — didn't attract the mysterious stranger. Finally she cut off a lock of her own hair, hid it under her mattress and went screaming to her parents. The subterfuge was soon uncovered.

Vamp: The Rise and Fall of Theda Bara

As she grew older and less obstreperous, Theda developed a taste for the theater, though theatrically minded children of the late 19th century had limited outlets for their ambitions. Most towns — certainly Cincinnati — had theaters, but theater-going was a special event. When bored by reading, friends and family gathered for parlor games.

One of the most popular amusements was the *tableau vivant*. Almost incomprehensible today, these "living pictures" were a source of entertainment through the 1920's. A successful tableau consisted of a group of people recreating a picturesque scene from a famous painting, play, or historical event, in great detail. Costumes, sets, lighting, and props were improvised with varying success and skill. The audience sat applauding politely as the curtain was drawn to reveal "William Tell Shooting the Apple from His Son's Head," "Caesar's Message to Cato," "Love in the Kitchen," "Women's Rights" (a 1901 classic consisting of "a domestic scene in which the duties of the sexes are reversed"), "Signing the Pledge" (a temperance scene) or countless other selections. They were also a much-debated and sometimes scandalous opportunity to appear half-naked in public, in the cause of historical accuracy. The tableaux were often accompanied by appropriate declamations of poems or readings.

Theda particularly enjoyed recitations, and bellowed forth with such popular selections as "Who Will Care for Mother Now?", "Casey at the Bat," and "Will New Year Come Tonight?" Her own favorite was a "pathetic" selection called "The Dirty-Faced Brat," which she was reciting endlessly for neighbors by the age of seven.

Bitten by the theatrical bug, Theda became violently jealous of a doll-like neighbor blessed with a melodic voice. Theda pushed the girl out of the way at one gathering and tore into song, while her mother cringed in embarrassment. Theda, however, knew no shame.

Theda's first appearance before a paying audience came during her grade school years. A neighbor — one Mr. Dyker — was persuaded to loan his barn to the neighborhood children. The Goodmans' Swedish maid (who, Theda tantalizingly said, later "went wrong") provided cookies and lemonade as bribes; children were charged "five pins" for entry. Marque Goodman acted as pitchman, usher and reverse bouncer, trouncing anyone who attempted to leave. There may have been many, for Theda was the solo star. "I sang, I danced, I recited," she proudly recalled.

Theda said she was "obsessed" by actresses by the time she entered high school. "I wanted to know how they dressed, what they ate, how they slept, and in short everything about them." Perhaps this grew out of her innate shyness, something she never really lost. As Theda told *Motion Picture Classic* in 1916, "I was afraid of making advances toward friendliness when I was a child. And as I grew up, this deepened. When other girls chummed together making fudge and going to parties, I was left out. And it made such a deep impression upon me that I am never the one to seek a friendship for fear I may be rebuffed."

In 1899, Theda entered Walnut Hills High School. The ornate stone building, erected in 1895, still stands today at Ashland and Burdett Avenues. Throughout her high school years, Theda affected black clothing, capes, mysticism, and took herself *very* seriously. She still socialized, however, working on the school's monthly newspaper, *The Gleam*. A neighbor, Leo Lemonek, remembered her as "tall, sort of skinny and full of devilment. I can remember she always wanted to be an amateur actress." Theda spent most of her free time at the Avon movie theater on Rockdale Avenue, enjoying the earliest of the silent films to hit her neighborhood.

Theda graduated from Walnut Hills in 1903 and enrolled in the University of Cincinnati (an unusual move for a woman of the

Theda (center row, far right) pictured with her high school dramatic club, 1903. She appeared in such light comedies as *The Lady from Philadelphia, American Beauties,* and *An Exciting Day. Below*: Theda (far right in gingham dress) with the staff of *The Gleam,* her high school newspaper (1903). *Photos: Walnut Hills High School, Kevin Grace.*

2 / The Lure of Ambition

THEODOSIA D. GOODMAN.
DRAMATIC CLUB; GLEAM STAFF
"With heart and fancy all on fire,
To climb the hill of fame."
Theo excels in the literary art, and her work bears the stamp of true genius. Her literary ability, however, is not the only claim she has to fame — her histrionic talent is a characteristic well known to those who have witnessed a performance of the Senior Dramatic Club. She is an entertaining conversationalist.

Theodosia D. Goodman's 1903 yearbook entry. *Photo: Walnut Hills High School, Kevin Grace.*

time). She spent two years attending classes, singing in the glee club and yearning for a stage career. Finally, in 1905, she dropped out and moved to New York, over her father's objections.

Theda Bara and the motion picture were both born in the 1880's. The birth date of both has been hotly contested; but happily, Theda's parentage was clearer than that of the movies.

For decades it has been universally accepted that Thomas Alva Edison invented the motion picture. He invented nearly everything else in the 19th century — and he certainly made a great contribution to the invention of film — but he's far from the sole father of the movies. As early as 1880, photographer Eadweard Muybridge was showing projected moving pictures. By 1893, Muybridge was exhibiting a "Zoopraxiscope" machine at the Chicago World's Fair.

In the 1880's, Frenchman Augustin Le Prince was also working on motion pictures, which he patented in 1888 (only a few frames remain today to hammer home his claim). Around the same time, George Eastman was experimenting with celluloid film. In 1893, Edison filmed his assistant Fred Ott sneezing; for some reason, it is

17

remembered as the first film. It all began happening very quickly after that.

Moving picture parlors swiftly became popular: you put a penny into the Kinetoscope or Mutoscope machine, peered into the hole, and a film loop lasting about thirty seconds flashed before your eyes. They weren't much; horses trotting, trains arriving, dancing girls strutting their stuff. Tiny plots began working their way into the loop, with titles like *The Athletic Girl and the Burglar* and *American Soldiers in Camp.*

By 1896, the motion picture was firmly part of the American consciousness. On April twentieth of that year, the public at large was introduced to the big screen. At Koster & Bial's Music Hall in New York (on the current site of Macy's), a dozen films were exhibited, including *Annabella's Butterfly Dance, Kaiser Wilhelm, Burlesque Boxing,* and scenes of Venice.

By the turn of the twentieth century, the basic technology of moving pictures was in place. As early as 1897, one Philadelphia theater was showing experimental talking films, and hand-colored films were not unusual. Some of the best came from France's Pathé Frères (*Sleeping Beauty*, 1903) and Georges Méliès (*A Trip to the Moon*, 1902). In America, films were being made which are now considered classics, including Edison's *Life of an American Fireman* (1902) and *The Great Train Robbery* (1903), both directed by Edwin S. Porter. Hundreds of now-forgotten films poured out, from delightful little comedies like *The Whole Dam Family and the Dam Dog* (1905) and *Mr. Hurry-Up of New York* (c. 1905) to dull, pointless films like *The Story the Biograph Told* (1903) and the almost unwatchable *Pounding Up on the Yeggman* (c. 1903). They rarely played in theaters for more than a day or two — one of unusual interest or popularity might run for a week.

By about 1910, most "photo-plays" were one reel in length (about eleven to thirteen minutes, depending on the projection speed). This allowed for a little plot development and a few camera tricks, but no real performances or scripts. This didn't stop the film companies from trying; such elaborate stories as *Uncle Tom's Cabin, Ben-Hur,* and *Romeo and Juliet* were condensed into ten-minute versions. *Ben-Hur* consisted mostly of a very unexciting and low-budget chariot race, and, much to film company Kalem's dismay, it was also the first film to be the subject of a copyright-infringement lawsuit.

Public interest in films (and the amount of money to be made from them) began raising the general level of the industry and its product. Two-reel films of about twenty to twenty-five minutes became more popular by the early 1910's, and finally, performers, directors, and cameramen were able to show off their art to appreciative audiences.

By that time, a few dozen established film companies were churning out entertainment, and countless smaller fly-by-nights were yapping at their heels. The American film industry was centered in the New York area, with Edison (established in New Jersey in 1894), Vitagraph (1896), Kalem (1907), Thanhouser (New Rochelle, 1910), Carl Laemmle's Independent Motion Pictures Company of America (or IMP, 1909), and Keystone (1912). In 1912, IMP joined with two other companies to form Universal. The best-known studio of that era is probably American Mutoscope and Biograph (founded in 1895), because so many of director D. W. Griffith's films have, happily, been preserved.

Healthy film companies existed outside New York, however, including Lubin (Philadelphia, est. 1897), Essanay (Chicago, 1907), and American Flying A (with studios in California and Chicago, 1910). Countless other companies flourished, produced hundreds of successful films, vanished in the silent era, and are all but forgotten today: Nestor, Rolin, Rex, Bison, Triangle, Selig; the list goes on and on. Dozens of "race" companies such as Micheaux, Norman, Florentine, Lincoln and Ebony employed black actors and workers, and filled a void for black audiences.

Vamp: The Rise and Fall of Theda Bara

By 1914, the film industry had grown out of its childhood. Films were increasing in length and complexity; four- and five-reel films of about an hour were being shown with short subjects, newsreels, and cartoons. Foreign hits like *Queen Elizabeth* (1912), *Quo Vadis* (1913) and *Cabiria* (1914) played alongside popular American films such as *A Tale of Two Cities* (1910), *Judith of Bethulia* (1913), and *The Spoilers* (1914).

The age of the film star was dawning as well, certain performers rising to the top like cream. They came from all walks of life. A few — very few — were established stage stars good-naturedly trying a hand at this new medium: Sarah Bernhardt, Anna Held, Maxine Elliott, James O'Neill, Lillie Langtry. Their film careers rarely amounted to much.

The great Eleonora Duse cancelled her film contract in 1916, saying, "if I were 20 or 30 years younger, I would start afresh in this field with the certainty of accomplishing much. But I should have to learn from the bottom up, forgetting the theatre entirely and concentrating on the special medium of this new art. My mistake, and that of many others, lay in employing `theatrical' techniques despite every effort to avoid them. Here is something quite, quite fresh, a penetrating form of visual poetry, an untried exponent of the human soul. Alas, I am too old for it!"

It was the lower rung of stage performers who made it big in films. Stock company and lesser Broadway players became the first real stars of the film. Florence Lawrence, Mary Pickford, Charlie Chaplin, Lillian and Dorothy Gish, William S. Hart, and many others left fledgling stage careers for undreamed-of success in the movies. They also brought some stage attitude with them: Maurice Costello was reportedly the first actor to put his foot down about building sets and being a good sport. He was a *star*.

Then as now, artists' models and fashion models were recruited by the film companies; that's how Pearl White, Norma Talmadge, Francis X. Bushman, and Mabel Normand made their ways to the screen. The industry was so loosely knit that even stagehands like teenaged Robert Harron found themselves in front of the camera.

During this period, several events took place which were to have a great impact on Theda's life and career:

• In January 1909, ten film studios banded together and formed The Motion Picture Patents Company, squeezing many small independent producers out of business. Many independents fought this tooth and nail in court. One of these producers was William Fox.

• In 1910, actress Florence Lawrence became the innocent subject of the first PR-inspired "movie riot." When she moved from Biograph to IMP, her new boss took advantage of a false death report in the newspapers to publicize her latest film. Lawrence's return from the dead caused such interest that she was mobbed at her next personal appearance. The movie business would never be the same.

• And in 1911, *Motion Picture Story*, America's first fan magazine, began publication. Soon, hundreds of writers, photographers, and editors were set loose, trying to outdo each other in grabbing readers' attention with fascinating, silly, fluff-headed, and sometimes insightful articles on films and their stars.

While the film industry was building up steam and making money hand over fist, Theda Goodman was struggling for a living in New York. She adopted the more exotic-sounding stage name Theodosia DeCoppet and rented a flat off Washington Square in artsy Greenwich Village.

Exactly what Theda did between 1905 and 1908 may never be known. Even after her career had ended and Theda was no longer spinning elaborate tales, she claimed, "I played legitimate roles in both the U.S. and England, and I had done very well — at least I was told so — in Shakespearean parts." In a 1919 article — perhaps written by Theda, perhaps not — she spoke mysteriously of "a year or two of weird incomprehensible experiences which are too intimate for the public eye," and time in Europe, in "one of those travelling, open-air companies that gave very poor Shakespearean performances." Not a scrap of evidence remains today to back up her claims, and those "weird, incomprehensible experiences" may have consisted of nothing more than pounding the sidewalks of Broadway looking for work, like thousands of girls before and since.

One writer has stated that Theda acted in stock with Mr. and Mrs. Charles Coburn (he was a Broadway star who later became a well-known character actor in films). Another reporter recalled seeing Theda around 1910, acting in one of New York's Jewish theaters on Second Avenue. But no such show titles survive with Theda's name in the credits.

Recalling his days in the DeMille Play Company in New York City around that time, Cecil B. DeMille remembered "rather wryly, the contracts that were not signed, as when I failed to take much notice of Theodosia Goodman although she used to come to our office hopefully when she heard we might be casting. She had to come to Hollywood and change her name to Theda Bara before she had her chance to add a new symbol, 'the vamp,' to American mythology."

She did find work in 1908. That summer, two productions of Molnar's *The Devil* were playing in New York; the more successful of the two starred George Arliss. Twenty-three-year-old Theda — billed as "Theodosia de Cappet" — was cast in Edwin Stevens' version at the Garden Theater. Theda appeared briefly in Act II as a party guest named Madame Schleswig. In a larger role, as an artist's model named Mimi, was a young actress named Marion Lorne who later gained fame as a radio performer and as Aunt Clara on TV's *Bewitched.*

Theda did not go on the road with Stevens' 1909 touring company, and vanishes again from sight until 1911, when she toured with the musical *The Quaker Girl,* at $25.00 a week. She didn't even make the lead road company with star Ina Claire, but the number two company that hit smaller cities like New Orleans. Actress-turned-gossip columnist Hedda Hopper first met Theda at this time, and later wrote that she "played a Frenchwoman, with an accent that wouldn't fool a five-year-old. Oh, brother!" Theda eventually dropped out of the show when her salary was cut to $18.00.

In the 1940's Theda waxed nostalgic about her stage career to theatrical manager Alan Brock: "Gradually one role after another led me to Portland, Oregon, where I was signed to do a complete season of stock. You know — September to June — and a new role each week. That was excellent training for a newcomer."

In 1912 Theda was still on the road, with "a frankly farcical play in three acts" called *Just Like John.* A summer hotel comedy, *John* never made it to Broadway. Trouping in a road company was no picnic, especially for a pampered child like Theda. Racing from train to theater, dressing in tiny crowded rooms, living in fleabag hotels with the cast, eating on the run. Theda later said that "I should like to blot this experience out, for it is full of disappointment and discomfort. I wanted to be an actress, to be sure, but I didn't want to be an actress at the expense of unpleasant associations. I came back to New York and in a little while my mother and sister joined me."

With no job and with no prospects looming — and with an unprofessional disdain for "unpleasant associations" — Theda's future did not look promising. Just when things couldn't get any worse, a fire broke out, destroying the Goodmans' apartment. Sensible Midwesterners that they were, Pauline, Theda and Lori had insured their apartment, and lived on the $900.00 insurance check during the winter of 1913-14. Theda later recalled "bringing the check home to my mother, crying copiously because it wasn't more, and saying to her at the time, `if I could only have cried like this to the insurance man, I should have got more money.'"

Theda had another problem to deal with: suddenly, her healthy hourglass figure was becoming unfashionable. When she'd hit New York in 1905, the biggest stars on Broadway were Anna Held and Lillian Russell, and Theda's curved, almost matronly figure was all the rage. But soon, fashion designer Paul Poiret and dancer Irene Castle changed everything. In 1908, Poiret banished the hourglass figure by introducing his sheath look: high Empire waistlines, tiny hips and pencil-thin skirts became all the rage. As Blanche Ring sang in *The Midnight Sons* (1909):

> Every lady's latest gown now, since 'way last fall,
> Must be worn straight up and down now, no hips at all!
> If we cannot have hips, why goodness knows,
> Fat girls can't wear any clothes!

The rise of dance team Vernon and Irene Castle in the early 1910's finally killed the full figure. Tiny, slim Irene became the nation's idol, and her bobbed hair and sylph-like appearance rang in the century of the crash diet. Theda, who loved her food and put on weight accordingly, suddenly looked like a behemoth next to the new generation of tiny young actresses with whom she was competing: Ina Claire, Hazel Dawn, Billie Burke. Always mature-looking, Theda could have passed for the mother of some of these girls.

By late 1914, Theda was pushing thirty and her career was going nowhere in a big hurry. After nearly ten years, she'd played no leading roles and hadn't even made a splash in bit parts. It was then that she met film director Frank Powell, who approached her with a line that was already old: "How would you like to be in the movies?"

Chapter 3

Her Triumph

By the summer of 1914, the film industry had entered its adolescence. Storefront nickelodeons were being supplemented by huge Picture Palaces, which were to reign supreme in the 1920's and 1930's (and which were so thoughtlessly torn down only a decade or two later).

By this time, nearly all "silent" films were accompanied by music. Even small-town theaters could afford a high-school girl to pound on the piano, if nothing else. Larger theaters employed professional pianists, three-piece bands or even orchestras. By the time Theda made her debut, it was unthinkable to show a film without musical accompaniment.

Films were generally not projected onto bed sheets or the pull-down screens we're familiar with from high school. Many higher-class theaters showed their films on bluish-white glazed bricks or even frosted glass, resulting in a beautifully glowing, liquid effect.

Patrons were no longer just the rowdy lower classes who could afford the nickel admission. Managers were doing all they could to attract the carriage trade as well, raising their prices and the quality of their surroundings. The January 1915 issue of *Motion Picture Magazine* is full of editorials, cartoons, and even poems emphasizing how respectable and educational films were becoming. Baby New Year is shown gazing at a horizon promising "reform dramas, Biblical dramas, current events, refined comedies." In another drawing, Father Time is shown inscribing in the book of the old year, "Motion pictures score another victory. Surprise world by great progress."

Vamp: The Rise and Fall of Theda Bara

Most studios had caught on to the star system and now publicized their players under their own names, except for Biograph (the joke went that Biograph employees had to surrender their names upon signing contracts; the names were kept closely guarded in a safe). Thus the Gish sisters, Blanche Sweet, and Henry B. Walthall were known to the public only by their faces.

But that day had passed for the most part. Leading ladies Mary Pickford, Clara Kimball Young, Alice Joyce and Florence LaBadie got enormous press coverage and thousands of fan letters. Other stars of the early 'teens included comics John Bunny and Max Linder and leading men Francis X. Bushman, Arthur Johnson, and Crane Wilbur. Pearl White shot to stardom in the 1914 serial *The Perils of Pauline*. Mack Sennett's Keystone comedies featured up-and-coming talents like Charlie Chaplin, Mabel Normand and Roscoe "Fatty" Arbuckle.

World events helped shape the film industry as well. In that summer of 1914, European nations fell one after another into war. Film production was no longer foremost in the minds of English, German, French and Russian pioneers, and America took the lead. The U.S. did not enter the war until 1917, giving them a three-year jump. Those were very important and eventful years for the film industry.

Theda said in later life that she'd scorned a film career and had to be dragged kicking and screaming to her first job. This is hardly likely. In 1914, Theda Goodman was twenty-nine years old and still largely unknown. Films were fast becoming a respectable living, no longer "galloping tintypes" viewed only by the great unwashed. Feature films of four or five reels were becoming popular, leading to more involved scripts and plots, and providing better opportunities for actors to get into their roles. Hopeful stars-to-be crowded dozens of East Coast studios for work: Lubin, Pathé,

Thanhouser, Universal, Vitagraph, Essanay, Famous Players, and Selig all had long lines at their gates by 1914, greeted by "no extras needed" signs. When Theda was approached by Frank Powell, her reaction was probably relief rather than disdain.

Her first action was in complete accordance with time-honored tradition in the acting profession: she lied about her age. When most successful film actresses were still in their teens, Theda would have been a fool to be honest. Primitive lighting, film stock, and make-up added years to even the most cherubic starlets, and a novice pushing thirty would have been assured the heave-ho. Theda adopted the birth year 1890 and stuck to it like glue. She also exaggerated her resumé, another tried-and-true job-hunting skill which has not lost its appeal.

Frank Powell was a somewhat successful stage actor who turned to film directing, working for the French Pathé Frères company until hired away by Fox in 1914 (he didn't stay long, decamping for Equitable in November, 1915). In the summer of 1914, he was still working at Pathé, directing a now-lost film called *The Stain*, on Lake Ronkonkoma, Long Island.

He knew he would soon be leaving for Fox, and he knew they were looking for a leading lady. It is not known exactly when or where he approached Theodosia Goodman. But it is certain that she made her screen debut as a bit player in *The Stain*. Powell placed Theda as an extra in a crowd scene. He put her close to the camera to see how she photographed and reacted to direction. He liked what he saw.

Throughout her career, Theda denied vigorously that this "screen test" ever existed: "I started out as a star and remained a star," she snapped whenever *The Stain* was mentioned. Little is known of the film; even the American Film Institute's widely inclusive catalog lacks a listing for it. Finally, in the 1940's, Theda cleared up the confusion and blithely admitted that she had indeed entered films as a lowly extra in *The Stain*.

While Theda and Powell were working at Pathé, thirty-five-year-old producer William Fox was preparing to make a film that would put him and his fledgling company on the map.

William Fox had been born in Hungary but was raised in the New York tenements. He began working in the garment district as a lining-cutter while in his teens, and spent the next few years struggling to make a living, obsessed with work and money, as many first-generation immigrants had to be. He entered show business in 1903 by purchasing a theater in Brooklyn and exhibiting motion pictures. Success followed, and before long Fox owned fifteen movie houses in Manhattan and Brooklyn. Soon he began building his own (the most famous is the still-standing Audubon, at 166th and Broadway, where Malcolm X was assassinated in 1965).

In 1907, Fox became a distributor as well as an exhibitor of films and the money continued to pour in. But two years later, The Motion Picture Patents Company was formed and created a stranglehold on the industry. No one could make films but members of the Trust. No one could lease films except from them. These ten companies decided that they, and no one else, comprised the American film industry. William Fox — and many other small businessmen — were on the outside looking in. Some independent companies fled to California where the weather was nice and the Mexican border a quick ride away. Others simply folded up and went bankrupt.

Fox was not one to take this lying down. He sued under the Sherman Anti-trust Act and won a large out-of-court settlement after a long, drawn-out court battle; the Trust was crippled by 1912.

William Fox. *Photo: Robert S. Birchard.*

With the money from his theaters and this lawsuit, William Fox began manufacturing his own movies under his own company, the clunkily named Box Office Attractions Film Rental Company (eventually to be known as Fox Film Corporation, and today, 20th Century-Fox and Fox Television).

Fox was like many of the early film makers: once hungry, from poor backgrounds, accustomed to pushing frantically for their goals. Not many of these men were well liked (Siegmund Lubin and Carl Laemmle being two unusual exceptions). Fox was a lot like Louis B. Mayer: a nice, fatherly man unless crossed. One of the few people with a kind word for him was composer Max Steiner, who described how Fox helped revolutionize musical accompaniment to films.

Calling Fox "one of the finest men the world has ever known," Steiner recalled how his career began. "I was the conductor at the Riverside Theater where we were showing a picture called *The Bondman*. I had an idea. Until about 1915 there was no special music written for motion pictures. We just used to take the albums publishers put out and would play `Hurry #1, Hurry #3, Love Scene #6.' I said to myself, `this is a lot of baloney. I'd like to do something new.' I talked to Mr. Fox and told him I wanted to write music for the picture . . . And I went down and wrote the music for William Farnum's *The Bondman*."

Fox's first effort was *Life's Shop Window*, starring Claire Whitney and Stuart Holmes. It was filmed on Staten Island and cost all of $6000. William Fox and his wife Eve set up a scenario department, costume shop, casting office and his own studios in Fort Lee, New Jersey, and Staten Island. A few more cheaply-made and moderately successful films followed. Then Fox purchased the rights to the scandalous stage hit, *A Fool There Was*.

A Fool There Was had taken a long, strange journey by the time William Fox began filming it in late 1914. The story actually began as a painting by Philip Burne-Jones (son of the more famous Edward) in 1897. "The Vampire," a scandal when first exhibited, had been heavily influenced by Bram Stoker's *Dracula*. It showed a white-skinned, black-haired woman leaning triumphantly over a prone young man, who'd either been drained of blood or sexually exhausted — it was all in the eyes of the viewer. It was a shocking view of powerful female sexuality: the painting gave men shivers and thrilled women. As a present to his cousin Philip, poet Rudyard Kipling wrote a popular, penny-dreadful poem, "The Vampire," to accompany the painting. It explained the young lady and her relationship to the victim from a distinctly male point of view: "The fool was stripped to his foolish hide," we learned, "So some of him lived, but most of him died." The public lapped it up.

This poem in turn inspired a melodramatic play (re-titled *A Fool There Was*) by Porter Emerson Browne, which premiered in New York in 1909 to great public success and equally great critical pans ("claptrap" was the term used by *The New York Times*). Tall, dark Katharine Kaelred starred as The Vampire on Broadway. The plot was now set: a diplomat is seduced from his family by an almost supernaturally evil woman. She was no simple sexpot; a good American family man could only be ruined by a vampire. Browne himself wrote a book version of the play that same year; it's hilariously awful (as are most quickie books based on popular plays and films). The book delved into the characters' backgrounds (The Vampire was an illegitimate gypsy, her victim a nice young WASP). The writing was terrible, containing passages like, "'Well?' he said of length in the French that is of Paris." The book died an instant death but the play continued successfully on tour.

William Fox, after purchasing the film rights to *A Fool There Was*, bided his time, amassing the money and talent to produce it. By late 1914 he had hired director Frank Powell away from Pathé and was set to begin casting.

Edward José had already been selected to play The Fool, John Schuyler. Indeed, José — who had worked with Powell at Pathé — later claimed he had discovered Theda himself, and that he directed much of *A Fool There Was*. The Belgian actor had been a stage and screen performer for years, with ambitions towards directing. Portly and greying, he seemed an odd choice for the leading male role.

The rest of the cast was auditioned and assembled. Schuyler's wife and daughter were played by Mabel Fremyear and Runa Hodges, neither of whose careers ever really took off. Stage actor

Vamp: The Rise and Fall of Theda Bara

Victor Benoit played Parmalee, an early victim of The Vampire's and the recipient of her soon-to-be famous subtitle, "Kiss Me, My Fool." Schuyler's sister-in-law was played by stage actress May Allison, in her film debut (Allison went on to a successful screen career of her own and died in 1989 at the age of ninety-eight). Frank Powell himself played the supporting role of a doctor and wrote the hour-long scenario.

But the main challenge was finding an actress to play the leading role — the film would stand or fall on her appeal. Fox later told his biographer, Upton Sinclair, "I consulted Robert Hilliard, who had produced it on the stage and played the leading role for years. He said, `In my experience, I have had to change my leading lady six times. As soon as one scored a tremendous hit in the part, she believed herself to be a Sarah Bernhardt and became unmanageable, and I had to let her go. My advice would be to put the girl you choose under contract, and the part will make her.'"

Fox had already considered and ruled out popular actresses Valeska Suratt and Madeline Traverse for the role. He rejected Virginia Pearson, who had taken over the Broadway role from Katharine Kaelred. Not deterred, Pearson went into films anyway. It was Pearson who starred in *The Stain* for Pathé, the film that launched Theda's career. In 1916, William Fox hired her as a second-string vampire, no doubt as a threat to keep Theda in line. Pearson, who came so close to having Theda's career, left Fox in 1919 to form her own company. Eventually shifting into character roles, she stayed on-screen until her retirement in 1932.

William Fox was beginning to get desperate in his search for a leading lady when Frank Powell brought Theda to his attention. At Powell's suggestion, Fox studied Theda's bit part in *The Stain*, interviewed the actress in person, and took Powell's suggestion. He signed her to a five-year contract, with yearly renegotiable options, at $100 a week.

Coming up with a name to put on the contract required some thought. In her stage career, Theda had tried at least six different variations of the deCoppet name — De Coppet, De Cappet, de Coppett, for instance — but her stage name suffered from a little too much mileage. At Fox's suggestion, Baranger, from the family tree, was shortened to Bara. Nicknames from childhood were surveyed: Theo, Teddy, and Theda. She decided to keep the latter; and thus Theda Bara was born.

After going over her contract with her mother and sister, Theda returned nervously to Fox's office the next day. According to her contract (and this was typical of the time) she would have to supply all her own non-period costumes. An actress without a ready wardrobe was in trouble, and most of Theda's clothes had been destroyed in the apartment fire. Realizing that she would have to buy seventeen outfits for her first film, Theda asked for, and received, a raise to $150 a week.

It's a good thing she got it, too: one particularly gullible reviewer noted that two of Theda's gowns in her first film were made of "real gold leaf" and "panther skin." That extra $50 must have come in handy.

Anytime a film "first" is cited, it's sure to be proven wrong: *The Jazz Singer* was not the first talkie by a long shot; *The Great Train Robbery* was not the first narrative film; and Theda Bara was not the screen's first vampire.

Eileen Bowser in *The Transformation of Cinema* notes Rosemary Theby in Vitagaph's 1912 *The Reincarnation of Karma* and a cigarette-smoking temptress in that same studio's 1913 *Red and White Roses*. Even *The Perils of Pauline* (1914) featured a raven-haired vampire threatening Pauline and her fiancé in one chapter.

Vamp: The Rise and Fall of Theda Bara

Alice Eis and Bert French perform the Vampire Dance in Kalem's *The Vampire*, filmed in 1913. *Photo: Robert S. Birchard.*

But the film which really knocks off Theda's claim was Kalem's *The Vampire*, made in 1913. As noted in James Card's *Seductive Cinema, The Vampire* starred Alice Hollister and featured dancers Alice Eis and Bert French recreating the Burne-Jones painting with their vaudeville-tested Vampire Dance. In fact, it may have been the success of this film that inspired William Fox to go ahead with *A Fool There Was*.

A Fool There Was began filming in the fall of 1914, with location shots in St. Augustine, Florida. Things did not start out smoothly: the company was hijacked by the British Navy just out of port. The *Fool* cast and crew had set sail on the German steam yacht *Essen*, and did not fly an American flag — two careless things to do in the

opening months of World War One. They were boarded by para-
noid crewmen of two British cruisers and Edward José was
addressed in German as a trap by a lieutenant. The multi-lingual
José answered him in kind and all hell broke loose. The trip was
delayed for several hours until Fox General Manager Winfield
Sheehan sent a convincing cable to the Brits and the *Essen* was
permitted to go on its way with full apologies.

Finally they arrived on location and Theda went to work in
earnest. "I shall never forget the terrible experience of my first
scene," she later told a reporter. "I had to wear a makeup in the
public street and I felt like a lost soul." It must be remembered this
was no ordinary makeup. The crude film stock of the time required
actors to get themselves up like clowns to register properly. Neither white nor red showed up well on film, so Theda had to appear
on that public street with a yellowish face, blackened eyes and
brown lips. She looked like the Living Dead; no wonder she felt
like a lost soul.

Screen makeup of the 1910's was by no means an exact science.
Film stock and variations in lighting equipment of the day necessi-
tated some experimentation; of course, some actors and studios
were more successful than others. Griffith's cameraman Billy
Bitzer was one of the best: he discovered that shooting outdoors at
the "magic hour" (just before sunset) resulted in the most flattering
final results.

Actress Mary Astor recalled what screen makeup was like
when she entered films in the 1920's. "Greasepaint came in a stick,
somewhat like a big lipstick," she wrote. "It was applied in streaks,
all over the face, and then smoothed until it filled every pore. With
a towel wrapped turbanlike around the head, you leaned over and
using a powder puff loaded with pinkish powder slapped it all
over until the grease had absorbed it. Really very similar to the
methods clowns use. Eyebrows disappeared, eyelashes were
coated, lips covered. Then it was all brushed off nice and smooth.

Vamp: The Rise and Fall of Theda Bara

Lipstick was a dark red. Reds went black on film, but if the tone was too light, one's mouth would look white."

It was even more primitive in Theda's day: the pink base Astor used still photographed brown in 1914, so actors in the early 1910's had to use a yellow base and medium-brown lipstick.

Theda's first scene, she recalled, "was taken on the steamship pier. There must have been 2,000 people standing around looking at me. The whole world seemed to have turned into human eyes . . . I trembled, I shook, I all but died right there on the dock."

Theda's disillusionment continued. She nearly quit the film when she discovered that one of her costumes was a one-piece bathing suit (women were still being arrested for indecent exposure in many towns for wearing these garments). "Now, I suppose I should have gone straight home again and starved nobly or ignobly, but I didn't," the pragmatic Theda later said. "Next day I reported with the one-piece bathing suit. It's all very well to say noble things about rather starving than debase one's art, but the butcher and the baker and the candlestick maker are not going to supply you with their commodities unless you are able to pay for them in cold, hard cash. Your flights of fancy won't bring you three meals a day." After all that aggravation, the censors objected to Theda's suit and it never made the final cut of the film.

Thousands of dollars were spent on the production: sets and costumes weren't stinted on. But re-takes were. *A Fool There Was* had to be ready for theaters as soon as possible, and Fox urged Powell to shoot quickly. This offered Theda no chance for rehearsals, for developing scenes, or even blocking out action. Powell would plunk her cold in front of the cameras and shout directions to her while cameraman Gene Santoreilli clicked away. Her theater training couldn't help her in this strange new world.

Even as talented and experienced an actor as John Barrymore found himself all at sea when making the switch from stage to silent film acting at about the same time. "I found that I overacted many of the scenes," he said. "Missing the stimulus of the audience I became indiscreet . . . the result was woeful and unreal."

In one scene, Theda had to pack her suitcase quickly while fending off a former lover. Her waist-length hair was streaming about her shoulders, and she wore a white, low-cut, sleeveless nightgown. Each time Theda leaned forward to throw something into the suitcase, her nightgown slipped down her shoulder; furious, she kept yanking at her gown while trying to carry on with the scene. Theda begged Powell to retake the scene so she could either let the strap fall where it would, or fix it so it would stay put. He refused, and her frustration is still evident on film.

There are other touches which a careful director should have caught: a car accident involving May Allison's character is so badly staged as to be hilarious, and Edward José's interpretation of delirium tremens resembles a grand mal epileptic seizure. However, Santoreilli's cinematography is breathtaking, especially for the period: a few vignettes involve lighting and set pieces as impressive as anything D.W. Griffith and Billy Bitzer were doing at the same time.

Theda felt her way through the new medium. In the early Florida scenes she appears stiff and self-conscious, pushing her lower jaw out in anger and moving her arms jerkily. But by the time the company returned to New York, Theda was catching her stride. She began loosening up, and her movements became fluid and snakelike, her facial expressions more natural. The film was edited quickly and readied for release by January 1915.

To make sure his film and his star made a splash, William Fox started laying plans while *A Fool There Was* was still shooting. He

Vamp: The Rise and Fall of Theda Bara

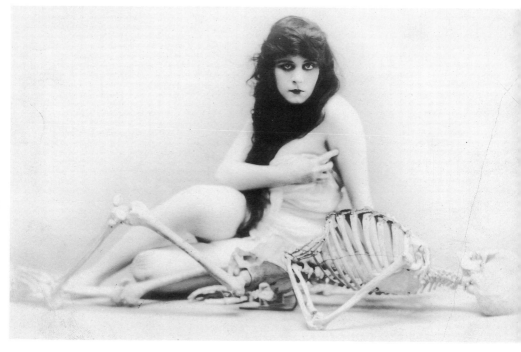

One of the more imaginative publicity shots from *A Fool There Was* (1915). *Photo: The Everett Collection.*

hired two newspapermen from *The New York World* whose enthusiasm approached dementia. Al Selig and John Goldfrap began setting the groundwork for the most lavish, ludicrous, and successful publicity campaign the country had ever seen. Eighty years later, many of these outrageous Selig/Goldfrap fables are still repeated as genuine film history.

The PR men knew that the film itself would only attract so much notice: the public had to become frenzied with curiosity about the previously unknown star if receipts were to roll in. To make matters worse, Edward José stormed out of Fox Studios after a contractual disagreement and refused to help promote the film.

It was left to the unknown female star to sell *A Fool There Was.*

Fox and his minions decided that "we had every type of woman on the screen except an Arabian; our publicity director felt that the public would like an Arabian . . . then the PR director said, `Now, let's not settle on this until we see if it will go over. Let me invite the newspapers to an interview and see if they will swallow this.'"

That's how the famous hoax press conference in Chicago came about. It all happened in early January, 1915, just before the pre-mière of *A Fool There Was*. The details of the afternoon have long since become a part of Hollywood legend: the recitation of Theda's Egyptian childhood and French successes; the dramatic appear-ance of the languorous, fur-bedecked star; her brief chat with the press, and her famously overheard cry of "give me air!" after everyone else had left.

But the press conference was never meant to be "successful." Selig and Goldfrap knew very well that hard-boiled reporters would take all this nonsense with a grain of salt. Some were already familiar with Theodosia Goodman's brief stage career. So they selected a reliable plant to report on the surprise denouement. Young Louella Parsons — not yet a famous Hollywood gossip columnist — was the one chosen to be on hand after the rest of the reporters had left. She witnessed Theda's real acting debut for Fox; ripping her veils and coat off, staggering to the window and throwing it open, gasping her assigned line. It was all planned and scripted to the last detail; the story was leaked to an amused world — as it had meant to be leaked all along. The press had been set up; the story had not been a *real* Arabian actress, but a *fake* one. It worked like a charm. As *Photoplay* put it, "little shop girls read it and swallowed their gum with excitement."

By the time 1914 had turned into 1915, the theatrical papers and gossip columns were either talking about the French-Arabian actress, or chiding the foolish papers that had fallen for the story. Theodosia Goodman gave interviews; Theda Bara turned them down. A great many non-New York papers, unfamiliar with Theodosia Goodman, swallowed the stories whole and referred to Theda as "the leading lady formerly of the well known Gymnase of Paris," and spoke of her costumes in *Fool* as having been designed by "the leading costumers of her native Paris." Goodness only knows where Theda actually got the costumes; probably one of the shops along New York's Ladies' Mile.

The rest of the press was proud of itself for seeing through Fox's publicity scam and adopted Theda. By the time *A Fool There Was* opened, Theda was already a celebrity, the girl of the moment.

A Fool There Was had a lot of competition; 1915 was a landmark year in film history. By this time, half of all American films were produced in California. Richard Rowland and Louis B. Mayer formed Metro Pictures Corporation that year, and D. W. Griffith, Mack Sennett and Thomas Ince banded together in the Triangle Film Corporation.

In February, Griffith's *The Birth of a Nation* opened, the first "great" (though, seen today, dreadfully racist) American film. Other 1915 successes included the scandalous melodrama *The Cheat* (with Fannie Ward and Sessue Hayakawa) and Vitagraph's *The Goddess* (with Anita Stewart, who was soon signed by Metro). An amazing array of stars made their film debuts that year: Billie Burke, Ina Claire, Victor Moore, Charlotte Greenwood, Elsie Janis, Jane Cowl, W. C. Fields, Vernon and Irene Castle, and Douglas Fairbanks. Comic Harold Lloyd was attracting notice; Charlie Chaplin signed with Essanay and released thirteen comedy shorts.

But *A Fool There Was* became one of the most popular films of that year. When it opened at New York's Strand Theater, an actor was hired to recite Kipling's "The Vampire" before the showing, presumably whipping the audience into a frenzy of anticipation. It seems to have done its job, as public and critics alike showered *A Fool There Was* and its star with praise.

Reviewers ignored the silly publicity and just critiqued the movie — and their opinions were almost unanimous raves. *The New York Dramatic Mirror* called the film "bold and relentless; it is filled with passion and tragedy . . . shot through by the lightning bolt of sex." The reviewer congratulated Fox for not tacking on a happy ending, all too common even in 1915. "Fortunately there is no such inartistic claptrap . . . the film remains true to its theme."

The same paper praised Theda's acting, as did *The New York Morning Telegraph*, which called The Vampire "quite the most revolting but fascinating character that has appeared upon the screen for some time." *The Pittsburgh Leader* mentioned her "intense dramatic realism," and *The San Francisco Call and Post* summed it all up by saying, "Theda Bara was an instant triumph."

She was also the first movie star to *become* an instant triumph. Nothing like this had ever happened, as commonplace as it is today. Several of Theda's contemporaries already had stage reputations when they entered the movies. But the rest had risen slowly, bit by bit, over the years. The public got to know their faces and nicknames: "The Girl with the Curls" (Mary Pickford); "The Fat Man" (John Bunny); "The Vitagraph Girl" (Florence Turner), but their names were a secret until well after their audience got to know and love them.

Theda Bara was the first film star to rise overnight from anonymity into superstardom. In the fall of 1914, she was an unknown actress. Four months later she was the world's most famous star. She was also the most reviled, which in itself added to her fame.

The success of *A Fool There Was* is not surprising; the plot was and remains a classic. Stories about evil women trying to debase good but weak men have always been big money makers. This basic plot has proven successful box office, from *Mata Hari* to *Gilda*

Vamp: The Rise and Fall of Theda Bara

Preparing to vamp, in *A Fool There Was. Photo: Wisconsin Center for Film and Theater Research.*

to *Double Indemnity* to *Basic Instinct* — few of which had the courage of *A Fool There Was'* unhappy ending.

Even a cynic like humorist S. J. Perelman admitted he was swept away by Theda's first film. "For a full month afterward," he later reminisced, "I gave myself up to fantasies in which I lay with my head pillowed in the seductress' lap."

The film finally put Fox on good financial footing. In 1914 he

In *A Fool There Was. Photo: Archive Photos.*

had earned a little over $200,000 in rentals; after expenditures he ended that year in debt. But — thanks mostly to Theda — Fox brought in more than three million dollars in 1915. Even after expenditures he cleared more than half a million. Not much by today's standards, but it enabled Fox to lay the groundwork for his multi-million dollar empire.

As the spring of 1915 settled in, William Fox realized with some alarm that he had no project ready for his new star. He quickly assigned her to co-star with stage actress Nance O'Neil in an already-planned version of the stage play *The Kreutzer Sonata* while frantically whipping his employees: writers, directors, and PR men were ordered to read books and newspaper stories, even watch other films for ideas. More vampire stories had to be readied for an immediate barrage on the American public.

Chapter 4

Her Double Life

Theda's second film — her first as a celebrity — began production early in the winter of 1915. If she was expecting star treatment on the set, she was in for a shock. William Fox knew when he signed her for *A Fool There Was* that she would become an instant star, and he wasn't about to let it go to her head. He remembered what Robert Hilliard had told him about suddenly famous actresses demanding raises. So, although he praised Theda to the rooftops in his press releases, Fox made sure she was treated like just another worker on the lot.

Along with co-star Nance O'Neil, Theda was assigned a new leading man from the Fox stock players, William Shay. A New Yorker who had appeared on Broadway and in films all over the world, Shay was one of many hard-working but largely unknown performers toiling for Fox. He appeared in four films with Theda before departing to the IMP company in 1916 and pretty much vanishing from film history.

She got a new director, too: thirty-five-year-old Herbert Brenon. The Dublin-born Brenon had acted in stock and vaudeville with his wife, entering films in 1909. He had hopped from company to company, eventually landing at Fox in time to guide Theda through *The Kreutzer Sonata* and three other films. He later went on to direct such hits as *Beau Geste, Peter Pan,* and *A Kiss for Cinderella.* Brenon was an enthusiastic professional, and enjoyed experimenting with new film techniques (while shooting one of Theda's films, Brenon shot one scene with six cameras, which was extremely rare in the 1910's).

Theda's second film was a trying experience for the new star;

Vamp: The Rise and Fall of Theda Bara

Herbert Brenon, who directed four of Theda's earlier films. *Photo: The Everett Collection.*

for one thing, she was in awe of and resented her co-star. O'Neil — rather intimidating at nearly six feet tall — had been on Broadway since 1896 and had played Lady Macbeth, Hedda Gabler, and Camille. She was a much bigger star than Theda and of course got top billing and kid-glove treatment.

The Kreutzer Sonata, freely adapted from Tolstoy, was fully as lurid as *A Fool There Was*. The story concerned Miriam Friedlander (O'Neil), an Orthodox Jew who cannot marry the father of her baby. She runs away with a violinist who is stolen by her wicked sister Celia (Theda). Miriam loses her mind and kills her sister, her husband and finally herself. The five-reel film, which ran about an hour, was very quickly filmed early in 1915, as Fox wanted to follow up on the success of *A Fool There Was*. Theda's second film was released in March, only two months after *Fool*.

When release prints, posters and press materials for *The Kreutzer Sonata* arrived at theaters nationwide, managers began displaying Theda's name on the marquees to bring in customers. Fox executives complained that O'Neil's contract called for top billing, but theater owners said it was Theda bringing in the crowds.

Years later, Theda spoke of her dissatisfaction filming this picture. "I was assigned to support a well known star," she recalled. "Again I was a `vampire,' and I was not particularly happy in the role. The studio became a factory, and I can think of no more applicable simile than to say we manufactured pictures in about the same way they make sausages. They were just turned out, one after another." Theda hadn't seen anything yet. By the time *The Kreutzer Sonata* was being released and reviewed, she was already hard at work on her third film, playing yet another vampire in *The Clemenceau Case.*

At least her *Kreutzer Sonata* reviews provided some good news: it was a big hit, mostly due to curiosity about Theda. "Startling and remarkable," according to one reviewer; another said of Theda and O'Neil, "their acting is splendidly realistic and emotionally powerful." Being favorably compared to a stage diva like Nance O'Neil must have given Theda strength to continue filming.

She needed it: the American public had no sooner digested *The Kreutzer Sonata* when *The Clemenceau Case* opened in April, 1915, Theda's third full-length film in four months. Based on a Dumas novel and once again directed by Herbert Brenon, *The Clemenceau*

Vamp: The Rise and Fall of Theda Bara

Case was the first film to star Theda entirely, with no famous co-stars taking up the slack. Unfortunately, Theda found herself playing exactly the same character as in her previous two films. As one newspaper put it, Iza Clemenceau "likes dimly lit rooms, the soft swish of oriental draperies, bizarre music and ultra-futuristic art."

Iza scandalizes her husband Pierre (Shay again) and threatens to ruin his best friend. Pierre — like Miriam in *The Kreutzer Sonata* — murders her and calmly calls the police. It seemed the happy ending enjoyed by The Vampire in *A Fool There Was* was to be a one-time-only event.

One of Theda's co-stars in this film, according to a press release, was "a giant king python — the largest of his kind in captivity," imported from the Bronx Zoo. The python, petted and adored by the wicked Iza, was cabbed from New York to Fort Lee by its "Hindu keeper" and Herbert Brenon. As *The Pittsburgh Leader* breathlessly related, the snake poked its head out of the cab on Broadway, and "men issuing from cafes fled back as they saw the alarming vision," while the Hindu played his pipe to calm the reptilian horror. Theda was widely praised for letting the snake wrap its coils around her.

The king python, of course, was about as dangerous as a wet sock. Stills reveal it to be the most unconvincing stuffed snake ever to appear before a professional camera. Theda seems barely able to keep a straight face as she clutches the toy to her in an attempt to keep it from falling to the ground with a thud.

A cleverer publicity scheme was enacted with the help of press-friendly lawyer Roy Hubbard, who claimed that one of his clients was inspired to kill his vampirish mother-in-law upon seeing *The Clemenceau Case*. The results of Hubbard's defense have been lost in the mists of time.

The film itself was largely lauded by critics and attacked by social reformers. One Rochester reviewer said of Theda that "not even her remarkable interpretation of the role of The Vampire in *A*

Fool There Was was more artistically done." Another called Brenon "the second best director of films in America" (one can only assume the first was D. W. Griffith), and stated that Theda "is destined to be one of the greatest of film stars." *The Fort Wayne Journal* added that "the theme and the acting of this brilliant woman grip and tense the emotions as but few other dramas have ever done."

Not everyone's emotions were tensed. One Philadelphia paper enjoyed Theda's acting but called co-stars William Shay and Stuart Holmes "slightly too repressed" and "colorless." Another paper felt that Theda "has overdone the matter of facial expression, as is commonly the case in moving pictures."

But the bulk of criticism was reserved for the lurid plot itself. The widely read and respected *Dramatic Mirror* praised both Brenon and his star ("too good to be engaged in picture production of this kind") but shot down *The Clemenceau Case* in no uncertain terms. "Were The National Board of Censorship possessed of any judgement whatsoever," the paper thundered, "this is the kind of a picture it should place the ban of its disapproval upon . . . no wholly pure minded man or woman could take a great deal of pleasure in witnessing such an exposition of female depravity."

As it developed, wholly pure-minded men and women must have been in short supply; *The Clemenceau Case* was an enormous hit. Released for three-day runs at most theaters, it was packed at every performance. The film opened in the pouring rain at the Broadway Strand, accompanied by a baritone, a fifteen-piece orchestra and "a rollicking Keystone comedy," to a turn-away crowd.

By this time, Theda was settling into a routine at Fox Studios and getting to know her co-workers. She was heading up a stock company of players who would support her in film after film for the next five years.

Vamp: The Rise and Fall of Theda Bara

There was her leading man William Shay; the darkly handsome, middle-aged Stuart Holmes, who specialized in villains; petite blonde second lead Mary Martin (not to be confused with the later musical comedy actress); British character actor John Webb Dillon; and child actresses Jane and Katherine Lee. One of the most talented Fox players was elderly character actress Alice Gale, who was often praised in reviews, even when she played minor roles.

Now that she was earning a regular salary, Theda moved into a large, airy apartment at 500 West End Avenue (at 84th Street), on Manhattan's fashionable upper west side. Then as now, West End Avenue provided large, imposing buildings, nearby parks, and a breeze from the Hudson River. Even after she left New York, Theda kept the apartment for her family and for her own East Coast visits.

Bernard Goodman remained in Cincinnati to look after his flourishing business, but her brother Marque joined Theda, Lori, and their mother in New York. Their apartment was furnished with quiet, clean good taste, much to Selig and Goldfrap's dismay. Press conferences with a French/Italian/Arabian vampire couldn't be held in this wholesome family atmosphere. One of the few reporters allowed into the apartment described it as "splashed with sunlight, warm and soft as heated water . . . modern in architecture and distinctly tasteful in detail. On the piano were strewn all sorts of musical compositions, with a generous assortment from Tschaikowsky." A maid, a Japanese houseboy and at least one pet dog completed the picture.

This, obviously, would not do, so the studio had to rent a New York hotel room for press conferences, bedecking it with crystal balls, incensed draperies, occult statuettes, and tiger skins. After the press left, Theda would change out of her vampire drag and go home to her family, books, and comfy furniture.

West End Avenue was also convenient to work. Fox's business

Theda at the Fox (Willat) Studio in New Jersey, ca. 1915-1916. *Photo: Robert S. Birchard.*

offices were in Manhattan, but his main studio was just across the Hudson River in Fort Lee, New Jersey (the Willat Studio, on Main Street and Linwood Avenue). The studio — like most at the time — was a huge barn of a building, covered not by shingles but glass plates for filtering sunlight. As many as a dozen indoor sets could be built, and as many movies made within the building at the same time. Theda might be emoting in one corner of the studio while — just yards away — Gladys Brockwell or George Walsh would be filming a scene for one of their movies.

Theda merely took a short ride up to the 125th Street ferry, then a trolley up Fort Lee's Main Street, to go to work. That ferry was full of film folk by 1915. Actress Blanche Sweet told *The New York Times* in 1977 that the commute was a delightful one. "I'll never forget the ferries. Never. I always used to get up at the bow of the boat . . . Going back —often it would be night time; the lights twinkling over in New York — with millions of dreams."

In the early- and mid-teens, the bucolic town of Fort Lee was one of the film world's capitals; sixteen studios were located there, producing nearly fifty percent of all American films. The situation was accelerated by New York City's distaste for movie companies. In late 1915, municipal authorities ordered all moving picture "factories" off Manhattan Island by January 1, 1916, declaring them a "public menace." Some took off for Fort Lee and other spots in northern New Jersey; others decamped to California.

Today, Fort Lee is a bustling commuter town, but in the early 1910's it offered a variety of advantages to film studios. The cliffs of the Palisades and local woods were perfect for adventure films, many of the streets looked like old western towns, and there were no telephone or electric poles to spoil a shot.

"Cameras were everywhere, grinding out dramas," a resident recalled decades later. "Burglaries and dynamite and fat men rolling down hills, and nobody even turned to look at them. Kindly old ladies didn't blink an eyelid when three galloping Mexicans were shot and killed at their very door." The kindly old ladies were no fools; Fort Lee became a boom town due to the film studios. Hotels and shops catering to the players sprang up, and one third of the local residents found work with the companies.

Today no trace remains of Fort Lee's former glory. By the 1920's nearly all the studios had moved to California because of the unaccommodating East Coast weather, and the shortage of workers and coal during World War One.

Theda had little time to enjoy her new apartment; in May, after a very brief break, she was shipped back to St. Augustine where she had begun her film career some six months earlier, to film Gabriele D'Annunzio's play *La Gioconda* (later re-titled *The Vampire* and finally *The Devil's Daughter*). Theda's new film was set in Florence, Italy, but St. Augustine was the closest Fox was willing to go to match exteriors. Theda's discoverer, Frank Powell, was called in to direct her for the third and final time.

When the company arrived in Florida, it was a broiling ninety-eight degrees, so everyone donned bathing suits and went down to the beach (Theda scandalized the locals with the same one-piece Italian bathing suit that had never made it to the final cut of *A Fool There Was*). Powell warned everyone to beware of sand crabs, and Theda laughed, "that's all right, we'll swim out into deep water." Then someone claimed to spot shark fins, and the easily terrified company scampered back to the safety of the hotel porch and some cool lemonade.

Other wildlife proved annoyingly uncooperative. One of the reasons Powell had come to Florida was to use the ancient Fort Manning as a location. When a guide told him the building was infested with deadly water moccasins, the unhappy Powell had to make other plans.

Theda began to discover what it meant to receive star treatment, if only on location. Even though her boss treated her like any other employee, Theda's fans were beginning to make themselves known. The company, staying at the Hotel Marion, was treated to

Vamp: The Rise and Fall of Theda Bara

Theda and Frank Powell (right) on the beach at St. Augustine during shooting of *The Devil's Daughter* (1915). *Photo: New York Public Library for the Performing Arts.*

a day trip by the Muller family, star-struck guests of the hotel. They took a launch to Summer Haven for a picnic, bathing, fishing, and paying a sightseeing visit to an old fort and a poultry farm.

All in all, filming *The Devil's Daughter* was an enjoyable experience, even if the storyline wasn't up to much. Theda was playing yet another vampire woman, impure of thought and rather vague as to motivation. Her character, an artist's model deserted by her fiancé, vows, "as this man has done to me, so do I henceforth to all men. My heart is ice, my passion consuming fire. Let men beware." She then goes out to raise hell, destroying several men before going mad in the final reel. It was all very operatic.

It was while making this film that Theda gained the nickname which put her into the dictionary. Her character in *A Fool There Was* was simply called The Vampire. Co-workers, reviewers, and Theda herself referred to the roles she played in *The Kreutzer Sonata* and

The Clemenceau Case as "vampire" roles. By the time *The Devil's Daughter* started filming, it was becoming an on-the-set joke, and the crew began affectionately calling Theda "vamp" as a nickname. She mentioned it to a reporter and it stuck.

Until 1915, a "vamp" was either a piece of stage business or music done over and over between acts (to "vamp until ready"), or the upper part of a shoe. But by the end of 1915 the word had entered the American vocabulary as "a woman who uses her charms and wiles to seduce and exploit men." Oddly, the term "flapper," so closely associated with the short-skirted, bob-haired girls of the 1920's, pre-dated "vamp," having been in common use since the turn of the century.

At first, Theda was proud of her new title and found it amusing and touching. After all, a joshing nickname meant acceptance by her co-workers. But within a year or two, she discovered that being labeled a "vamp" was as restricting a harness to her career as Mary Pickford's "Girl with the Curls" and Charlie Chaplin's "Little Tramp."

When she returned, sunburned and happily exhausted, to New York in mid-June, Theda discovered that acting was only part of her new job as a movie star. Al Selig and John Goldfrap sat her down and explained a few things: in order to keep up public interest in the new star, Theda would have to perform off-screen for reporters when not performing on-screen for moviegoers.

Every few days, she was supplied with slinky satin and fur-trimmed dresses and sent to Fox's exotically decorated hotel suite. Selig and Goldfrap coached her with scripts for the interviews and gave her several pieces of schtick to use over and over. She generally had to pull out some "ancient" piece of jewelry and tell its weird history.

Vamp: The Rise and Fall of Theda Bara

Among these trinkets was a locket containing a painting of her father which Theda supposedly found in a thrift shop in Mulberry Street. It had been stolen from her mother, she said, in Italy. Theda happily rushed in to purchase it and wired her mother — "working for the Red Cross in Paris" — that the piece was back in the fold. Another was her precious Amen-Ra statue. "When I was a little girl, my mother was walking me past a curio shop in Paris," Theda elaborated, "where these were on view in the window. I wanted them because I recognized them in an instant . . . I sleep with them. They are always concealed about my clothing when I am acting."

At one of her first interviews, she surprised reporter Nixola Greeley-Smith with a serpent bracelet. With a perfectly straight face, Theda told The Tale of the Bracelet to Smith, who dutifully passed it on to her readers. "An East Indian Gaekar had given the actress a wonderfully wrought snake bracelet containing an Indian poison," Smith wrote. "Mlle. Bara was showing [a] young man the secret spring by which the poison was released from the mouth of the hollow gold snake when he suddenly seized it from her and, placing it to his lips, died at her feet!"

Theda, who had dutifully memorized her script, expounded on her vampire theories to Smith. "I think most vampires are dark women," she purred meaningfully, "though some have blood-red hair and green snake-like eyes. [Authoress] Elinor Glyn is a good specimen of this type physically . . . I have never loved, and if I ever fall under the spell of a man, I know that my power over men will be gone!" Oddly, this last pronouncement came perfectly true years later.

To promote *The Devil's Daughter*, Fox had Theda claim she was personally chosen for the role by author Gabriele D'Annunzio, who was then living in Europe. "I first met D'Annunzio when he came to Paris to put on a playlet of his at the Théâtre Antoine," she lied prettily. "D'Annunzio insisted that I should play the leading role in his sketch . . . When I was cast for the same part in *The Devil's Daughter*, I wrote to the poet asking his views of the character. I received in reply a voluminous letter giving detailed instructions . . ." The reaction of D'Annunzio himself, if he ever read these stories, was never recorded.

Selig and Goldfrap also distributed a publicity release calling Theda — much to the bemusement of her childhood friends and neighbors — "The Wickedest Woman in the World." Playing on the popularity of reincarnation theories, the release claimed that "scientists have questioned [Theda] to secure fresh evidence to support their half-proved laws of transmigration of souls, of reincarnation of personality."

One newspaper, displaying portraits of Lucretia Borgia and Delilah, claimed that the souls of these ladies, along with 17th century mass murderess Elizabeth Bathory, had come to rest in this "half-Italian, half-French" actress. When questioned on the subject, the paper said, "Mlle. Bara cannot answer." As Theda herself later noted, she was probably laughing too hard to answer.

Significantly, some papers were not fooled by all this nonsense. As early as May 1915, one Cincinnati paper proudly trumpeted the fame and success of their "Local Movie Actress."

Even a few successful artists were dragged into the fray. Magazine illustrators Charles Dana Gibson and James Montgomery Flagg were paid by Fox to sign their names to a press release singing Theda's praises. After rather unpleasantly describing Theda as a woman "whose lips scorch like living fire and whose kiss is destruction," the artists got down to business. "Never have I had a model who impressed me as deeply as Miss Bara," Gibson supposedly said. "In her dark eyes lurks the lure of the vampire; in her every sinuous movement there is a pantherish suggestion that is wonderfully evil." Flagg's statement smacked equally of Selig and Goldfrap: "Mlle. Bara is unique. I do not believe there is another woman on earth like her."

Theda's being called one of the world's most beautiful women raises more than a few eyebrows today, when her looks are considered rather plain and bovine. She had a heavy jawline and rather cumbersome nose ("Bourbon," she called it). Even in her day she was thought a few pounds overweight. And she disproved the motherly advice that "everyone looks better smiling." Theda's thin-lipped smile merely pushed her chin out further and made her eyes squint.

Some of this has to do with changing styles in beauty: actresses Florence Lawrence and Mabel Normand were considered great beauties in their day but wouldn't turn heads in the late twentieth century. But photos really don't do Theda justice. In motion pictures, her mobile features somehow came together into a very pleasing whole; when she spoke and moved, her large chin and nose somehow faded into insignificance. True, she could never be compared to some of the classic beauties gracing the screen in the 1910's, like Lillian Gish and Norma Talmadge. But Theda in person and on film put photos of her to shame.

When *The Devil's Daughter* was released in June 1915, reviews were generally good and all mentioned those lovely Florida "Italian" exteriors, although some complained of lack of close-ups. *Moving Picture World* called it a "wearisome" and "laughable" imitation of *Fool*, but *The New York Review* said it was a "wonderfully good picture . . . Miss Bara's enaction of the title role is perfect." *The Sunday Telegraph* said that "her facial expression is fascinating in its brutality and cynicism and her every movement is one of physical allurement."

Fans loved it, and her: one paper noted that "Theda Bara is getting to be another Mary Pickford" in terms of popularity, if not sweetness. "Her picture on a poster outside is a guarantee of a crowd inside."

But Theda had more than fans and critics to please. When *The Devil's Daughter* was released, The Ohio Board of Censors demanded that 1800 feet be eliminated, almost excising its star from the film.

As far back as the 1890's, social reformers and religious groups fretted about the effect of films on the masses. In 1908, the Mayor of New York tried (unsuccessfully) to shut down all nickelodeons in the city; the following year, The National Board of Censorship was formed. This didn't stop states, cities and even small towns from forming their own censorship boards, with their own whimsical rules and regulations. Police chiefs and church leaders stormed theaters if a possibly offensive film was being shown. It was impossible for film makers to please them all. One Major Funkhouser of Chicago was notable for his strict censorship, and was to have many run-ins with Theda (she once offered to meet him on a trip to Chicago; he haughtily refused). The Pennsylvania, Ohio, and Kansas Censorship Boards (the first three to be formed) were particularly well-known for hacking films to bits.

Cuts ordered in Theda's films by the Kansas State Board of Review are typical:

- All scenes of Theda's smoking and drinking were either cut from *Gold and the Woman* (1916) or were shortened to "flashes."
- In *Cleopatra* (1917), all scenes of "suggestive advances of Cleopatra on Caesar," and all close-ups of "exposed limbs" were ordered cut.
- Important scenes were either cut or shortened in *Salome* (1918), including Salome visiting John in his cell and

Salome kissing John's head on a platter.
- Suggestive titles, including, "I admit it, Dearest Elsie, I intend to keep you here for myself" were axed from *When Men Desire* (1919).

Fox was faced with a dilemma. Theda smoking, drinking, showing her limbs and luring men to destruction was what brought audiences to the theater. Plots had to be framed to excuse Theda's actions, or a moral had to be tacked on the end of her stories to make her "pay the price." For the next few years, Theda's screenwriters danced on a tightrope trying to please audiences and censors alike. Critics, however, and Theda herself, were often dismayed by the results.

Significantly, Theda's next film was the first in which she didn't play an out-and-out villainess. The plot was a well-known one: *Lady Audley's Secret* had been a standard of the melodrama stage since the novel was published in 1862. The film was shot at the Life Photo Studio in Grantwood, New Jersey, with Marshall Farnum directing. Theda played Lady Audley, a respectable, wealthy wife and mother who believes her husband is cheating on her. She herself has an affair, then shoves her lover down a well when he threatens to expose her (the body in the well being the "secret" of the title). In Theda's version, her "dead" lover, not badly hurt at all despite his trip to the bottom of the well, reappears, causing poor Lady Audley to lose her mind.

In midsummer 1915, Theda's constant requests to the front office were granted, and she was given the chance to play her first genuine heroine, no vamping involved. The vehicle was yet another nineteenth-century penny-dreadful melodrama, *The Two*

Orphans. The Two Orphans was the tale of wealthy foundling Henriette, left on the doorstep of a poor couple who already have a daughter, Louise. Louise goes blind, and the two girls endure all kinds of horrific adventures before being rewarded with a happy ending.

The story had already been filmed at least once: Kathlyn Williams and Winifred Greenwood had played the sisters in Selig's 1911 production. Of course, the version best known today is D. W. Griffith's 1922 *Orphans of the Storm,* starring Lillian and Dorothy Gish. A French Revolution sub-plot was added by Griffith for additional drama; it did not exist in Theda's version.

Theda was assigned the role of the brave heroine Henriette, while the put-upon, blind Louise was played by Jean Sothern, a stunningly beautiful blonde actress. Sothern, only twenty when she co-starred with Theda, had been in show business since childhood and was already an established vaudeville and film star when Fox signed her. Sadly, her career was a short one. She fell ill with cancer in 1921 and died three years later at the age of twenty-nine.

Herbert Brenon was brought back in to direct *The Two Orphans,* part of which was filmed in Quebec. The shoot was like an extended vacation: Quebec in the summer was a glorious place to be, Theda felt comfortable with the pleasant and very professional Brenon, and — despite the creakiness of the project — she was happy that Fox was finally allowing her to play a heroine. She felt a little self-conscious about Jean Sothern's overpowering beauty, but there was nothing to be done about that. Brenon, still suffering from acting fever, cast himself as the evil hunchback Pierre, who abuses Louise frightfully until meeting a well-deserved end.

While the crew was still filming *The Two Orphans, Lady Audley's Secret* opened to mixed reviews and lukewarm box office receipts. *The New York Mail* ranked *Lady Audley's Secret* "very high when considered with the general run of features being presented," while another paper called the film "weird and thrilling." Theda, though, received unstinting high praise. *The Detroit Free Press* noted that "no star has a greater following among picture fans," and added that as Lady Audley Theda "displays . . . real magnetism combined with stellar acting qualities . . . Her depiction of the gradual growth of the mental distress that wrecks her mind and finally makes her raving mad is a fine type of character acting."

More than one critic noticed the money Fox poured into sets and costumes: "You have to marvel at the lavish hand which sets his stages and wonder how his bank account can stand the drain upon it."

Theda dutifully pasted these notices in her scrapbook when she returned to New York in late summer, but the front office kept her all too aware that critics couldn't get audiences into theaters. Fans were disappointed at seeing Theda sinned against rather than sinning and business fell off sharply.

When *The Two Orphans* opened in early September, Fox did a minimum of press agentry. The picture all but sneaked in and out of theaters, with only a few reviewers taking note of it. Those few reviews, however, were favorable, lauding Theda for unsuspected talents. "To change from a sinuous vampire . . . and become a gentle innocent young girl, would seem like a hard thing to accomplish," said *The Detroit Free Press*, already a champion of Theda's. "The result shows what a powerful, versatile actress can accomplish."

But business was dreadful. Fox claimed it was because audiences wanted to see Theda vamping again; Theda countered that *The Two Orphans* had received little promotion and was doomed to fail. The fact that *The Two Orphans* opened in the sweltering late summer — the slowest time of year for films before air conditioning—could not have helped. Privately, she suspected that Fox had torpedoed the film in an effort to get her back into her sure-fire money-making vamp roles. She may have been correct; her next film, unpromisingly, was entitled *Sin*.

To rehabilitate Theda's reputation as the living embodiment of evil, Emily H. Vaught, "New York Society Phrenologist and Physiognomist," was called in to give her impression of Theda's "bumps." Up until the 1920's, many people still believed that personality could be read by the shape of one's skull or physical peculiarities. Vaught went to town on Theda.

"Theda Bara has the muscular system of a serpent," Vaught exclaimed. "Never in all my experience as a professional character reader have I gazed into a face portraying such wickedness and evil — such characteristics of the vampire and the sorceress." The press release even included sample "exclusive" interviews for newspapers to reprint, complete with a blank space for the reporter to fill in his or her name.

When Theda was supposedly being gazed at so intently by Emily Vaught, she was actually hard at work on *Sin*, her first gangster film. Her co-stars were William Shay and Warner Oland. Oland, born in Sweden, had been a successful stage actor and was just beginning his long film career. By the time of his death in 1938, he had starred in scores of films, most notably his Charlie Chan series.

Theda portrayed peasant girl Rosa, "a daughter of the passionate Italian soil," who is seduced by New York mobster Pietro (Oland). She follows him to New York, trailed by her loyal lover Luigi (Shay). Poor innocent Luigi steals The Jewels of the Madonna during the Procession of Our Lady of Mount Carmel and goes mad with the realization of his crime. Rosa, not to be outdone, goes mad as well and all ends unhappily.

Disaster nearly struck during filming. Brenon needed footage of the annual Procession of Our Lady of Mt. Carmel in lower Manhattan. He took a studio car, camera and cameraman, Theda, and William Shay, and piled them off to location. Brenon and the cameraman shoved the bulky camera atop the car, while Theda and Shay relaxed and chatted inside, enjoying their front-row seat for the parade. Suddenly, the car's roof collapsed, and the two men and their machinery tumbled inside. Luckily, Theda escaped with some minor cuts and bruises, and filming went on.

Sin was another huge hit, helped by good reviews, the fact that it was banned in Ohio and Georgia, and ads that predictably read, "Sin with Theda Bara!" The poor showings of *Lady Audley's Secret* and *The Two Orphans* were barely perceptible blips in Theda's career, and didn't affect her popularity at all. Indeed, as the autumn of 1915 wore on, it seemed as though her fame was just starting to pick up steam. She had her first *Photoplay* cover in August; the cover blurb called her "an ingenuous little girl, intellectual, almost bluestocking at times." To make up for that all too accurate view, Theda was featured on the cover of the notorious *Police Gazette*, the 1915 equivalent of being a *Playboy* centerfold.

Photoplay followed up their cover with a lengthy interview in their September issue, imaginatively titled "Purgatory's Ivory Angel." Reporter Wallace Franklin claimed he was a cynic regarding Theda, that he enjoyed Fox's publicity hand-outs even though he knew what nonsense they were. "I prefer to disbelieve those stupid people who insist that Theda Bara's right name is Theodosia Goodman, and that she is by and from Cincinnati," he wrote.

From that time on, few could pretend to be ignorant of Theda's true background; Franklin had spilled the beans in one of the nation's most popular new fan magazines. Yet even he let himself be bowled over by Theda's brilliant performance at their interview. He found her in Fox's new Jersey City studio, recently purchased from Pathé Frères. The studio itself, Franklin wrote, was a "delightful quadrangle of yard and building, poised on the west shore of the Hudson River . . . a picture studio such as the fans most often imagine, and most often isn't."

Theda's sweet and home-like dressing room, said Franklin, contained "a plain little couch, littered with those soft drowsers our grandmothers called `sofy pillows.' There was just space for a chair or two; a dressing-table with powerful lights and fine glasses . . . — and la Bara."

La Bara poured it on for Franklin, repeating her stock childhood tales of pyramids and French theaters, and debuting another story which she'd repeat — with slight variations — for years. "I was walking near my home in Manhattan," she began earnestly. "I had a big red apple in my hand, and ahead of me I spied a little girl with thin legs, a faded calico frock, and oh, such a hungry look! . . . I put my arm around her and put the apple in her hand, and she looked up with a frightened, happy little laugh. Then her eyes fell on my face, and a look of terror came into hers. She stumbled backward, away from me. I was frightened, too. Other little girls came up. `It's the vampire!' whispered the biggest, in a croaking way. Then they all ran, and I went home and sobbed like the littlest of them."

Franklin — and several other reporters — fell for the story and reprinted it, even though several children sensibly wrote to fan magazines saying they'd have asked Theda for her autograph if they'd recognized her, rather than running in terror.

The only time Theda dropped her script and spoke from the heart was when Franklin mentioned her vamp roles. "Oh, please, please don't call me a vampire," Theda groaned. "I believe that I am inherently an *actress*, and I like the adventuress because she has color and intensity. Do you understand?" No longer the world-weary man killer, Theda became a frustrated *artiste* as she pleaded, "I wish to the uttermost depths of my soul, for a part in which I'd neither be an incarnation of evil, as I am now, nor an incarnation of holiness. I want to play a kind-hearted, lovable, human woman. Won't someone write me such a part?"

Not while William Fox saw how successful Theda Bara was as a vampire, they wouldn't. He was too busy thinking up new schemes to sell her to the public as that incarnation of evil. *The Cleveland Plain Dealer* was persuaded to hold a look-alike contest. The official "Theda Bara of Cleveland" (and winner of five dollars) was Miss Beatrice Gold.

Another bit of imaginative, around-the-bend press agentry was a syndicated write-in contest, asking readers why they would — or wouldn't — marry Theda. The answers, on the whole, were surprisingly level-headed and showed that Theda's fans could make the distinction between the actress and the role. One "Miss ISG" from Mississippi wrote, "that a sweet, wholesome woman like Theda Bara should make such a good vampire on the screen merely proves her gifted with unusual powers." That clipping got an honored place in Theda's scrapbook.

A few months later, Theda gave an interview to widely syndicated writer Archie Bell, who also began his piece by calling her "little Theodosia Goodman of Cincinnati, Ohio." She told him another version of the terrified child story, this time with a happier ending. Theda bought a "fine basket of fruit" for a group of children and they shrieked in terror upon recognizing her, but this time, "I called them to me and talked with them; and finally, we became friends."

The frightened child story was only one of many legends about Theda which were re-circulated — with slight changes — through the years. Another concerned a woman who kicked a hole in a poster of Theda outside a theater, happily paying ten dollars for the damage, claiming, "it was worth it!" Wacky fan (and non-fan) letters were invented for the public's entertainment. One was from an Oriental gentleman requesting a photo of the "honorable Theda" as "honorably naked as possible." Another was from a furious wife claiming, "it is such women as you who break up happy homes." That straight line led Theda to answer, "I am working for a living, dear friend, and if I were the kind of woman you seem to think I am, I wouldn't have to."

By the close of 1915, Selig and Goldfrap's version of Theda's childhood had been thoroughly discredited; even her densest fans were put wise. Later writers claimed the Arabian birth tale was implicitly believed throughout her career, but actually, it lasted less than a year and was looked upon with great skepticism from the beginning. By February, *Photoplay* was regularly referring to Theda as a Cincinnati girl, and in January a syndicated writer revealed her origins as well. "All sorts of lurid pasts have been painted for her," he wrote, "but it is said they existed only in the versatile imagination of the press agent. In reality Miss Bara is a wholesome, healthy girl who enjoys the same things that appeal to other young women of her age."

The public loved it and felt very superior for having seen through the tales all along. Theda continued rattling on about crystal balls and palmistry in her interviews, but Guiseppe Bara and Theda de Lyse were finally laid to rest. Theda herself played dumb. When asked point blank her place of birth, she batted her eyes prettily and said, "And what, pray, has that to do with my art? Is it not enough that I am here?"

At the same time that Theda was gracing all those magazine covers, she was handed her first "prestige" film, *Carmen*. Fox wasn't at all put off by the fact that Cecil B. DeMille was planning a competing version which would feature the film debut of popular opera diva Geraldine Farrar.

Theda's *Carmen* was based on the 1845 novel by Prosper Mérimée, while the Farrar version stuck closer to Bizet's opera;

both plots incorporated bull fights, knife fights, and fist fights. Theda certainly seemed good casting: Carmen was described by Mérimée as a black-haired, black-eyed gypsy: "It was a wild and savage beauty, a face which astonished you at first, and was never to be forgotten. Her eyes especially had an expression, at once voluptuous and fierce, that I have never met since in any other human glance."

Theda had something entirely new in director Raoul Walsh. The twenty-eight-year-old Walsh was referred to as "a maniac" by no less than two separate reporters, one of whom also noted his "Rabelaisian sense of humorous filth." His enthusiasm was appreciated, but the calm intellectual Theda was somewhat put off by Walsh's constant hyperactivity. John Goldfrap, an occasional on-set visitor, noted that Walsh suffered frequent temper tantrums and kept a supply of cheap pocket watches to "dash into a hundred pieces against a convenient wall."

Goldfrap's presence on the set was appreciated by Theda, if not by visiting journalists. When E. Arthur Roberts asked Theda on the *Carmen* set if she was a Cincinnati native, she smiled, "I wonder who circulated that story? Where was I born, Mr. Goldfrap?" "Egypt," Goldfrap smiled back.

In order to compete with Geraldine Farrar's *Carmen*, Walsh — who also wrote the film's scenario — decided to emphasize action, often at the expense of plot, motivation, and character development. He bluntly told one reporter, "my main object was to put plenty of action in it. I saw to it that there is something doing every minute the picture is on the screen . . . I write my own scenarios, and I cut all my own pictures." Walsh also ascribed his success to the fact that he and cameraman George Benoit shaved their heads for good luck on the day they started each film. It must have worked, as Walsh went on to much greater successes, including *The Thief of Bagdad, What Price Glory?, High Sierra,* and *White Heat.*

Filming was exhausting for Theda and her co-stars, who

Raoul Walsh, who directed Theda in *Carmen* and *The Serpent*. *Photo: The Everett Collection.*

included Swedish actor Einar Linden in his American debut, and Fay Tunis as Carmen's enemy, Carlotta. Tunis was recruited from New York's Spanish immigrant community and thrown into a fight scene with the star. Theda got somewhat carried away by Walsh's directions, which consisted of tearing off his coat, jumping up and down and screaming, "Go at her! Get her down! Scratch her! Bite her! Good!" "What a terrible woman," Tunis muttered about Theda as she limped off the set, never to film again.

Einar Linden, witnessing Tunis' fate, blanched when asked to do a fight scene with Theda, which was supposed to climax with his fall from a forty-foot balcony. A stuntman was procured from the extra ranks — with the promise of more pay—and Theda whaled away at him until he tumbled off the railing to the mattresses waiting below. Linden was relieved that he'd chickened out.

Fox spent an estimated $30,000 recreating Seville in Fort Lee. Press handouts claimed that authentic matadors, picadors and banderillos were shipped over from Spain for the film (along with one Andalusian bull), but there's no way to prove that extras weren't simply pulled from the ranks and given fancy uniforms.

Theda herself drew the line when Walsh handed her a peasant costume: old rags from a thrift store. A well-brought-up young lady, "I couldn't wear anything that anyone else ever wore," she shuddered. "I bought nice, clean, new fresh goods and took it into my kitchen and ran a horse-radish grater over it," she laughed to a reporter on the set. "Isn't it as ragged as anyone could wish?"

Theda had other problems on the set besides old clothes and terrified co-stars — Raoul Walsh's fiancée, actress Miriam Cooper, was extremely jealous of any actress who worked with her man, and was particularly irked by Theda. "She was coarse, overweight and unattractive," snapped Cooper in her autobiography, still furious after half a century. "I thought she was terrible. Her only expression was to duck her head and stare at her leading man with what appeared to be a searching look."

Cooper elaborated on that "searching look," claiming that Theda was blind as a bat. She was quite right: Theda was extremely nearsighted and helpless without her hand-held lorgnettes (which were more easily hidden than glasses when photographers came snooping about). Theda learned to be very careful: she planned ahead, going over her lines and marking out the furniture, props and camera lines with her lorgnettes. Then, when the time came to go through it "blind," she was able to work from memory and not do a Keystone over the sofa.

4 / Her Double Life

Miriam Cooper was no one to be trifled with. When *Carmen* had its press preview in October, 1915, Theda wasn't told of the event. The only woman present was Miriam Cooper. Walsh's girl-friend also had no love for William Fox: she mimicked his accent and said that he tried to tack a happy ending onto *Carmen*: "You don't vant the audience should valk out with a bad taste in their mouth." Cooper's story is somewhat suspect, as Theda already had six less-than-happy endings under her belt.

Cooper especially looked down on Fox compared to D. W. Griffith (she appeared in Griffith's *The Birth of a Nation* and *Intolerance*). "You can't compare the two men," she said. "Mr. Griffith is an artist and Mr. Fox is a businessman." Of course, she had a point. Theda would have given her eyeteeth for a project as fulfilling as *Intolerance*.

Griffith himself was more sympathetic than Miriam Cooper. He claimed to be an admirer of Theda's, and — with a jab to his rival William Fox — told a reporter that "no actress, not even Bern-hardt, could have saved some of the vehicles handed Miss Bara."

Both Fox and DeMille felt it would be good publicity to play up a feud between their Carmens, and snappish interviews with Theda and Geraldine Farrar began appearing as the two films were readied for the theaters. "Men are like cakes," Farrar told Nixola Greeley-Smith. "The one with the pink icing still on the bottom of the bag always seems more delectable than the one with the green icing out of which you have taken a bite."

Smith then ran across town to get Theda's views. "Are men cakes?" Theda sneered. "If they are, even a child knows . . . that the difference between the cake one has nibbled and the cake in the bottom of the bag is principally in the imagination of the cake-eater."

That's as personal as it got; the actresses never progressed beyond cakes to critiquing each others' performances. Theda, of course, suddenly discovered that she'd lived in Spain in one of her many previous lives. "I have felt a strange sensation whenever I have thought of this girl Carmen of the Spanish hills," she sighed mystically, having memorized Selig and Goldfrap's latest interview script. "It seems to me I knew all these events — even before Mérimée — that I was Carmen herself."

This particular reporter took Theda's entertaining rambling with a grain of salt. *The Cleveland Leader* reporter had previously dismissed her childhood tales with, "apparently they put baby Theda on the back of a camel and sent her to Paris to grow up." But the same reporter was impressed by the enthusiasm Theda showed in putting forth her story. "No actress on the stage ever acted so perfectly as she acts off the stage."

Dropping the company line, Theda became somewhat more human and discussed her ambition to return to the stage someday: "It is my greatest desire that people shall hear my voice from across the footlights. . . . All my work is seen by audiences when I am home in bed, or working at some other picture. You smile about my being home in bed while other people are at the theater? It is true; my maids will tell you."

The life Theda led while working sounds less like a glamorous film star than that of a small-town school teacher. After a tough day's work, she said, "I get into the automobile, go home as quickly as possible, my maids give me a little warm milk or a light lunch and I go to sleep and rest until far into the night. Then I feel like myself again and study and read." Theda told another reporter who asked if she enjoyed swimming and riding that "I'm indolent; I'd rather lie on a hammock, or on my couch, and read." As writer Emily Belser later put it, "beside her, Greta Garbo was a screaming magpie."

The two *Carmen*s opened in November and both did very good business, though critics generally proclaimed Geraldine Farrar the winner. Typical was this view: "After the living, breathing Carmen of Farrar's creation, that of Theda Bara seems as insubstantial as a

Above: Theda as Mérimée's "wild, savage beauty" in *Carmen* (1915). *Photo: Archive Photos. Below:* Horace B. Carpenter, Geraldine Farrar, and Billy Elmer in Cecil B. DeMille's version of *Carmen* (also 1915). *Photo: Robert S. Birchard.*

shadow, although doubtless the moving picture star would shine with far brighter radiance were a lesser luminary than the American Prima Donna placed in juxtaposition." Another reviewer groused that "I was never particularly fond of wild, stary eyes. They give me the creeps," and added — somewhat ominously for Theda's career — that "it's impossible to associate Theda Bara with anything except a vampire, even off the stage."

But some reviewers were impressed, not only with the Fox sets (which "conveyed a very real Sevillian atmosphere"), but with Theda herself ("there is no mistaking the fact that she is one of the best motion picture actresses in the country"). Theda's *Carmen* did quite well at the box office; booked for three-day runs in most large cities, it had to be held over in many. In Illinois, fans were told that "it would be well for those who would be sure of gaining admittance to come early and to see the film in the daytime," and in Louisville thousands were turned away from packed houses. In Springfield, the film was held over, and the local paper noted that "six days is indeed all too short a time to enable the public's interest in this unusual production to be met."

Censors in Harrisburg, Pennsylvania certainly preferred the Fox version: they held up and cut Farrar's *Carmen* and passed Theda's, leading horrified reviewer Charles Bregg to state that "there is a wide difference between sensuousness and sensuality — a difference the French [sic] actress should be taught, and censors should be wise enough to observe."

Theda was anxious to be rid of Raoul Walsh and Miriam Cooper when she started filming her next movie, *The Galley Slave*, in late summer, 1915. Fox agreed to assign Walsh elsewhere and gave Theda over to J. Gordon Edwards, Fox Studio's production head, as temporary director while lining someone else up for her next project. The forty-seven-year-old Edwards (step-grandfather of director Blake Edwards) was born in Montreal and started his career as a British army officer. Switching to the theatrical profession, he moved to New York and became an unsuccessful actor and a successful director. In 1910 Fox hired Edwards and shipped him overseas to study European film-making methods. Tall, rather cadaverous, and distinguished, he was just the sort of unflappable intellectual Theda adored. The two got along like a house afire.

Edwards loved directing the big picture: he doted on elaborate sets, crowd scenes, and lighting effects. Like Alfred Hitchcock, he hired talented actors and gave them free rein. "I believe that the less directing a director does, the better the picture will be," was his philosophy. "Let the actress do a scene in her own way, let her have a chance with her temperament — that has always been my idea. Then you obtain grace, naturalness, the living thing, the thing that makes pictures as well as drama."

"I read the scenario once," Edwards continued, "then I throw it aside and never look at it again. A slavish following of its dictation would hamper me at every turn, making that which should be fluid and living into something static and dead." This laissez-faire attitude may have made for good relations with actors (though not screenwriters), but it also left Theda on her own as far as characterization went.

A talented actress, Theda nonetheless needed a firm hand. She and Edwards thoroughly enjoyed working together, but his directing style sometimes left her at loose ends. Theda was probably speaking of J. Gordon Edwards when she later reminisced, "one time I asked my director about a certain scene. Do I repulse the advances of this man, or do I lead him on? `Oh, just keep the audience guessing,' he said."

She quickly learned to rely on others for specific direction. "My camera man is my artistic speedometer," she said in what could only be taken as a slam at directors in general. "If he likes a scene I know it is good; if he shakes his head — sometimes I cry a little because I am so tired but I always do a re-take."

The Galley Slave was the extremely complicated story of Francesca Brabaut, who is wronged by her evil husband, falls in love with an artist and finally enjoys a happy ending. Adapted from yet another Victorian melodrama, it was quite a comedown from *Carmen*. It was a year before Theda would be handed another worthwhile role. Till then, it was back to vamping. Theda tried hard to underplay the role of Francesca, which was noted by several reviewers. One stated that she emerged from the film "with flying colors," while another called Theda's performance a "tremendous dramatic triumph, splendidly acted." Theda herself was more appreciated than the film, which was generally thought rather confusing and lackluster.

Her next film was lurid enough to make up for any timidness in her previous offering: her character in *Destruction* lived up to the title, bringing a business, a town, and most of its citizens to ruin in little more than an hour of screen time. As Ferdinande Martin, Theda played the gold-digging wife of a Pennsylvania foundry owner, who vamps both her stepson and a union leader, bringing on no end of family and labor problems. J. Gordon Edwards was unavailable for the next few months, so Theda had to work with other Fox directors, this time Will Davis, who took the company to Pennsylvania for location shooting in mid-autumn.

A lucky — for Davis — accident occurred when the old Kingsdale mansion, a local tourist attraction, burned to the ground. Never one to let an opportunity slip by, Davis filmed the blaze and incorporated it into the film's finale. He had Theda's character hiding from the vengeful workers in her home, which is accidentally torched; she and the union leader perish miserably, as the camera cut back to exteriors of the Kingsdale mansion burning.

Ferdinande Martin plots the downfall of an entire town in *Destruction* (1915). *Photo: Wisconsin Center for Film and Theater Research.*

One writer felt the ending "proves what her film friends have long feared for Theda — that she would one day suffer spontaneous combustion and go up in smoke."

Destruction was released somewhat inappropriately on Christmas Day, 1915. It was one of those films that was so bad it was good, and did excellent business. Theda was ludicrously wicked as Ferdinande; audiences cheered rather than booed when she brought the town to its knees. Theda tore into the role like a puppy with a rag in its mouth, and even critics were impressed: "The Vampire of the Screen was never better," said one reviewer, adding somewhat generously that "the play is a masterpiece both for production and for the acting of Miss Bara." *The Cleveland Leader* proclaimed that "the acting is of the same high order that characterizes Miss Bara's work."

By the time *Destruction* opened, Theda was filming yet again, this time an expensive production set in Russia. "That young lady must be working day and night," wrote Archie Bell. "Perhaps we are getting accustomed to it, but it is worth recalling that she appears in a brand new photoplay every few days."

Her first 1916 release — again directed by the bumptious Raoul Walsh — was *The Serpent*. Theda was cast as Vania, a peasant girl engaged to a nice young man (George Walsh, the director's brother), but seduced by a Grand Duke. Vowing revenge, she becomes the sweetheart of the Russian nobility, destroying the Duke's son and finally the Duke himself. "We have serpents on the Steppe," Vania tells her seducer, "harmless unless you tread on them — and they strike to kill!" Not a few critics noted plot similarities to the recent Broadway hit *Within the Law*.

Walsh went all-out on the locations, filmed in the dead of winter in New Jersey. Vania vamps her way from Russia to Paris to London, and thousands of dollars were poured into both interior and exterior shots, as well as military costumes and huge crowd scenes. Walsh pretty much left Theda to her own devices, wanting this to be a Raoul Walsh — rather than a Theda Bara — film. He introduced a wild boar and an owl into the plot (the latter bit Theda on the hand) and incorporated battle scenes (in which several extras were nearly blown to bits by prop land mines and had to be carted off to a Fort Lee hospital). When the season's first snow fell, Theda was called upon to trudge haplessly through the Jersey swamps and forests towards the Duke's palace. Walsh was never one to let a picturesque snowfall pass him by unfilmed.

The Serpent was released in January 1916 and promptly rejected by New York censors who claimed that Theda's character should not be permitted to triumph, even if Vania's actions were somewhat forgivable under the circumstances. Fox, bowing to pressure, hastily tacked on a cop-out ending in which Vania tumbles out of bed, discovering that — surprise! — it was all a bad dream and she was still an unsullied peasant girl. Less easily cowed towns than New York could simply leave off that last reel and enjoy their vamping unapologetically.

Theda was particularly hurt that *The Serpent* was rejected by The Catholic Federation in her own home town. In a self-serving but heartfelt press release, Theda complained that "I cannot conceive why my appearances in the Cincinnati theaters could give grounds for the protests now being published . . . Every mother, every minister, every person with the well-being of the younger element of Cincinnati owe me gratitude for what I have accomplished through these pictures." Theda knew what nonsense this was, but, furious at the pompous and hypocritical religious fanatics in Cincinnati, signed her name to the statement with a flourish.

Partially due to the scandal, the film did very well — in fact a Rhode Island theater had to suspend ticket sales because it sold out so quickly. Many of Walsh's touches were appreciated by critics: "The photography has rarely been excelled and seldom equalled," wrote Archie Bell. "There are big battle scenes that in many moments compare to the pictures in *The Birth of a Nation*." Walsh's much-beloved low-comedy touches, however, went over like a lead balloon. "His managers," said Bell, "should call a halt on this vulgarity, to save the goose that lays the golden egg."

Theda's personal notices were decidedly mixed. *The New York Review* called *The Serpent* "the best thing Theda Bara has done," but *The New York Mail* carped that "Theda is rather a sneering heroine in this dramatic picture, making frequent use of the curling lip and the wicked eye." Not everyone was taken in by the location shots, either. Even Theda's champion, Archie Bell, had some fun at their expense. "Our heroine of the Russian New Jersey marshes goes off to Paris (Fort Lee)," wrote Bell, "where she watches the soldiers returning from the front (the Hudson River ferry)."

Some reviews, mentioning her typecasting, gave Theda pause: *The New York Times* said that same month, "since Miss Bara is so well fitted by looks to act this sort of creature before the camera, it would be squandering her resources to cast her in a Mary Pickford sort of role." "Box office receipts from Coney Island to the Golden Gate prove that the public wants her to be a vampire," wrote Bell, "but how long can she keep on the same track?"

She certainly kept on the same track in *Gold and the Woman*, yet another vamp programmer. Directed by James Vincent, it boasted a very complex plot spanning several centuries of American Indians and Spanish settlers. Refreshingly, the film took a sympathetic view of Native Americans and the invasion of Europeans: all this was soon swamped, though, when *Gold and the Woman* switched to a modern-day story of Juliet De Cordova (Theda) taking vengeance on the descendent of a Spanish Conquistador. In the heated finale, Juliet — after leaving a trail of dead and dispirited men in her wake — dissolved into a view of Satan himself, effectively tinted red on the film stock.

Gold and the Woman was Theda's first film to be written by Irish-born scenarist Mary Murillo, who had previously worked at Éclair and Universal. Murillo worked on another four films with Theda, after which Adrian Johnson took over most of the scenario duties. Theda also worked with scenarist Mary Asquith. It wasn't at all unusual for women to write films in the silent era; women had a surprisingly powerful place in the film industry in the 1910's. Successful ladies behind the camera included directors Alice Guy Blanche, Lois Weber, Margery Wilson, and Nell Shipman, and writer/directors Frances Marion and Jeanie

Looking very unhappy about her unflattering makeup in *Gold and the Woman* (1916). *Photo: Wisconsin Center for Film and Theater Research.*

Macpherson. Even actresses Mabel Normand, Kathlyn Williams, and Grace Cunard tried their talents as directors (Normand, in fact, directed many of Charlie Chaplin's early films).

But even as powerful a woman as Theda Bara couldn't go over the heads of local censors: New York, Cincinnati and Cleveland boards turned *Gold and the Woman* down flat. Fox lost revenues in those three cities, but was smart enough to publicize the censorship, thereby causing a box office rush in other towns.

Critics hated the film: *The New York Review* laughed that "it

Vamp: The Rise and Fall of Theda Bara

Out for a drive in 1916. *Photo: New York Public Library for the Performing Arts.*

would pay an enterprising undertaker to camp on Miss Bara's trail," citing the number of men she destroyed. But Theda's latest director, Bertram Bracken, managed to get a quiet, measured and intelligent performance from her, and even her harshest critics were impressed.

Some were already beginning to take William Fox to task for wasting his biggest star in such unworthy films. "What is Fox going to do with Theda Bara?" editorialized *Photoplay*. "This woman is not only one of the country's biggest drawing cards, but she is a worker. She has brains, ambition, willingness to learn." Most critics, able to tell the difference between bad acting and bad writing, were coming to Theda's defense.

Chapter 5

A Good Little Devil

The true definition of a "star" is someone who will pack the theaters no matter what the vehicle. By mid-1916, Theda was a huge star; her legion of fans still rushed to see her, no matter what critics said about such dross as *Gold and the Woman* or *Destruction*. Theda herself made the evening worthwhile and sent them home satisfied. That season, she was voted the country's fifth-most-popular actress, after Clara Kimball Young, Anita Stewart, Virginia Norden and Mary Pickford. She even had a sandwich named after her: minced ham, mayonnaise, sliced pimento and sweet pickles on toast. Served warm, of course.

Long before Elizabeth Taylor or Cher had signature perfume, Theda had a scent created by "perfume artist" Ann Haviland. The fragrance (not, sadly, called "Vamp") consisted of woods and gums of Persia ("to typify her Orientalism") and pomegranate blossoms ("typifying the depth of her soul and radiating warmth"). The results, according to the *Columbus Dispatch* reporter, were "subtle and hunting" (one can only assume the typesetter left the "a" out of "haunting").

Thousands of fan letters from around the world poured in to Fox Studios every week. Theda didn't have time to answer them all, though she saved each and every one, pasting favorites in her ever-growing scrapbook. Fans sent drawings, gifts, and, in that long-ago time, reams and reams of poetry. "Probably more poetry is written about Theda Bara than any other subject in the world except 'Spring,'" sighed one newspaper, under the headline, "Theda Bara Fans Are At It Again." Theda's scrapbook is overflowing with hand-written poems sent by her fans. Mary E. Caldwell "respectfully submitted" this selection:

Vamp: The Rise and Fall of Theda Bara

> Ah! Theda you're the greatest "vamp"
> The world has ever known
> You've traveled through two hemispheres
> Where other "stars" have shown
> And yet you hold an asset
> Far beyond the art of "sin"
> Of a better truer nature
> Than the "pictures" show you in.

Beatrice Billing of Minnesota was a little more down-to-earth in her contribution:

> Theda Bara in stripes is a winner,
> And makes a most excellent sinner;
> Yet in real life they say
> She finds thrills quite passé —
> And even eats onions for dinner!

From limericks to heroic verses, the poems continued to arrive throughout her career, as did pleas for money and favors. One poverty-stricken old woman wrote to Theda of her life-long desire for a boudoir gown and cap. "It amused me so that I sent her *two* caps," Theda later said. Requests for money, film roles, and marriage were forwarded to Fox's publicity men to deal with.

In the spring of 1916, those publicity men came up with a scheme which was to outlive them, and Theda, for decades. Newspapers were eager for exclusive interviews, but there were only so many hours in a day. So Selig and Goldfrap wrote a series of autobiographical articles with Theda's byline and distributed them to local papers around the country. *The New Orleans Daily State* ran them as "written especially for *The Daily State*," *The Newark Star-Eagle* ran them as "written especially for *The Newark Star-Eagle*," and so on. The series was written, supposedly, to reassure censors and religious reformers that Theda Bara was a home girl at heart.

Ever since 1916, film historians have quoted these articles as Theda Bara's own words and opinions, despite the fact that she herself later disavowed them. Not only didn't Theda write the articles, she didn't even proofread most of them before they went to press. Each morning, she and Lori would sit over their breakfast of coffee and sausages and "roar with laughter" at each new chapter in her autobiography. "I read so many lies about myself that I hardly know what is the truth anymore," Theda later said. She was amazed at the gullibility of the public and thought some of the stories "were so wild that we didn't think they would be printed, or that if they were printed, they wouldn't be believed. But they were printed, and they were believed, too, I suppose. The wildest press stories were the most successful ones."

Theda took it all with a grain of salt and didn't let the tales get her down — in fact, the only thing that really got under her skin was the lack of good roles being thrown her way. As long as she was enjoying herself as an actress, the antics of the press squad merely amused her. The solemn girl from Walnut Hills High School had learned to laugh at herself, and in the long run, that saved her sanity.

Theda Bara was one of the few sex symbols to survive the experience intact. "A sex symbol is a heavy load to carry when you're tired, hurt and bewildered," said Clara Bow, Theda's successor in Hollywood. Bow, Errol Flynn and Marilyn Monroe found themselves so sucked into their identities as sex symbols that their own personalities became submerged and stunted. When their careers began to fade, when middle age loomed, they found themselves unable to live life offscreen. Their personal lives crumbled because they took their professional lives too much to heart.

The survivors were people like Theda, Jean Harlow, William Haines; people able to distance themselves from their fame and develop outside interests: family and friends (Harlow), a second career (Haines), a sense of humor and perspective (Theda).

Theda's chatty, sweet-hearted autobiographical series ran for several months, on subjects like what nice, normal interests she had ("afternoon teas, spiced with a bit of gossip, perhaps. Shopping, with luncheon in an attractive tea room"), what young men wanted in a bride, and what she herself wanted in a groom ("when he smiles the joy of that smile must travel to his eyes").

The Atlanta *Constitution*, not taken in by the fraud, published a wicked parody penned by "Theda Bearcat," which confessed that "there is some ominous fate that stalked in my path when I was but a young girl trying to get along. It clutched me by the throat, dragged me aloft in its murky clouds, stifled my good resolutions and put me in pictures at a salary of $1500 a week. I sincerely hope no other girl shall be preyed upon in this fashion." This spoof has also long been quoted as Theda's own writing.

Genuine interviews still appeared; reporters showed up at Theda's dressing room fully expecting a good show. Rowland Thomas interviewed her in 1916, and began the chat by requesting not to be vamped. "I'm off duty now," Theda laughed. When Rowland asked what vampiring was like, she set him straight. "Make-believe vampiring such as I do seems to be mostly plain hard work. It means hours and hours before the camera every day. The only holidays are when it's rainy. The only sports and recreations I get time for are my bath and change of linen."

When not laughing up her sleeve at Selig and Goldfrap's latest harebrained schemes, Theda was, of course, hard at work. Her third release in 1916 was *The Eternal Sapho*, very loosely based on Daudet's scandalous novel. In this film Theda played yet another artist's model (her third and far from her last), who is swept from her poor but humble Greenwich Village existence to become the darling of the Bohemian set.

As bad as the film itself may have been, Theda did a bang-up job in it, getting rave reviews. *The Louisville Times* called it "the crowning work of her wonderful film career." John De Koven of *The Cleveland Leader* had previously thought that Theda "did not act — merely grimaced, posed and made herself generally objectionable." But now, he had to admit, "she acts. And she also touches you on the heart, something the old Theda could never do." One newspaper went so far as to say that the only other star in a class with Theda was Charlie Chaplin.

Yet another moth-eaten melodrama provided Theda with her next film. By 1916 *East Lynne* was something of a joke. The 1861 best-seller became such a hit onstage (even Theda's rival Nance O'Neil had played in it) that by the turn of the century, countless stock companies and traveling players were putting on their own pirated versions, each one more lurid than the last. It even became a catch phrase: when someone was acting overly dramatic, friends rolled their eyes and said sarcastically, "next week, *East Lynne*."

East Lynne was the story of Lady Isabel, who falsely believes her husband has been stolen by a rival. After being disfigured in a train wreck, Isabel returns anonymously to act as her own children's governess, finally dying in her repentant husband's arms. Released in June, *East Lynne* did surprisingly well for such an old chestnut. "All those who were fortunate enough to see this feature were loud in their praise," said *The New Britain Herald*, and reviews were pretty much along this line. Critics praised Fox for casting Theda as a heroine: "Miss Bara has shown . . . that she can play other roles than `vampires,' said one paper, "and do them just as well . . . Mr. Fox showed excellent judgement in choosing her for this role." Considering the actresses who had played Isabel over the decades, it was no small compliment when *The Detroit Free Press* said that "few of the older heroines surpassed [Theda] in emotional depth."

East Lynne is one of the few Theda Bara films to survive (a 16mm print was purchased from Fox by New York's Museum of Modern Art in 1971). Viewing it today provides a mixture of delight at seeing a long-lost Bara film and pain that such a mediocre example was chosen for survival.

Bertram Bracken tried to cram the entire 473-page novel into one hour of film time, retaining every sub-plot and minor character. People unfamiliar with the novel or play *East Lynne* will be baffled by the film, as explanatory subtitles are stinted on.

Theda is a charming Lady Isabel, underplaying most of her role with sincerity and naturalness. It's only in the heavily melodramatic moments that she gets carried away; in particular her death scene looks like a parody of silent film acting. She clutches her heart, her eyes bulge, she claws at the air and collapses on a conveniently placed sofa. Bracken seemed unable to rein in villain Stuart Holmes, as well. Like Theda's, Holmes' performance veers from understated and effective to outright ham. Additionally, Bracken's idea of irony is as delicate as a sledge-hammer: when the villainous Holmes is trying to convince Theda that her husband is untrue, the camera cuts away to an actual snake in the grass.

For *East Lynne*, Theda had to transform herself from a vamp to an innocent heroine — not only psychologically, but physically as well. In these early days, actresses were responsible for their own hair and make-up. Theda's stage training did little good here, as screen make-up was a new and developing art. Harsh lighting and primitive film stock made even dewy actresses look middle aged, and Theda's features were particularly susceptible to unflattering shadows and angles. Her strong chin, prominent nose and thin lips made her appear downright plain if the cameraman — in this case, Rial Schellinger — wasn't very careful. Like many actresses with

As Lady Isabel in *East Lynne* (1916). *Photo: The Everett Collection.*

deep-set eyes, Theda needed a low-set light to bring them out.

Schellinger's camera work in *East Lynne* is fairly impressive. The outdoor scenes apparently were filtered to soften the light, and the elaborately set indoor scenes were beautifully attended to. Close-ups, long shots and interesting camera angles are evident throughout the film. Even double exposures are used as two ghosts appear to haunt startled cast members.

Theda was no make-up artist, so she eventually hired a maid who became expert at painting her boss. "For some roles I have had to be literally painted white," Theda told *The Boston Post* in 1920. "My maid always did this; and I told her once that if she ever left me she could certainly get a job at whitewashing, for she'd had plenty of experience. Getting rid of this white afterward was not easy; but it was nothing compared with the ordeal of removing the brown I used when I played a dark part. Two or three baths were sometimes needed to take off this color."

Theda's maid must have been quite good at her job, as one reviewer noted in 1916 that Theda "can apply make-up so skillfully as to obtain excellent results, something quite rare in filmdom." In *East Lynne*, however, someone dipped a bit too enthusiastically into the lip rouge. As the sweet Lady Isabel, Theda's mouth was far too severe and dark and her eyes a bit too kohl-rimmed.

The costumes in *East Lynne* are obviously expensive, but of indefinable period. The ladies' panniers and fichus look vaguely eighteenth century, although the action takes place in the time of telephones and automobiles. And the haphazardness of Fox's prop department becomes evident when Lady Isabel disguises herself to return home (Bracken changed the book's plot, not wanting to disfigure his star). She simply dons a pair of dark glasses and a hideous horsehair wig and no one knows who she is. Theda's mother, the ex-wigmaker, must have been appalled.

All in all, *East Lynne* is not the best film by which to judge

Theda Bara's career. But for all the pedestrian plot and sometimes uneven acting, Theda's star quality stands out. Surrounded as she is by a loyal and hard-working cast, she owns the screen. When Theda appears, everyone and everything else seems to fade from view.

After the favorable reviews and acceptable financial return on *East Lynne*, Fox bowed to Theda's pleas and cast her in another non-vamp role. He chose *Under Two Flags*, a popular novel by Ouida which had become an even more popular Broadway show in 1901. After playing "musical directors" for the past few films, Theda was reunited with J. Gordon Edwards. The two worked together so well that they became a team: her next twenty-two films would be guided by Edwards.

Filmed in the early summer and released in August 1916, *Under Two Flags* was shot mostly in Montauk Point, Long Island, standing in for Algiers. "It was just like getting home again," Theda sighed to a reporter. "I was born at an oasis in the Sahara. I felt as if I were returning home from a long, long trip when I found that Algeria was the setting for my latest picture." The reporter knew perfectly well by now what nonsense this was, but it was a good joke and he played along. The story appeared verbatim and deadpan — amazingly, a few papers were still printing Theda's Fox ancestry, and a few fans still actually bought it.

Under Two Flags was the story of the daughter of a French Foreign Legion member, who goes by the name of Cigarette. The pet of the company, she falls in love with Englishman Bertie Cecil who, through various plot twists, is sentenced to the firing squad. Cigarette obtains a pardon, arriving on horseback just as the order to fire is being given. As the Fox press handout puts it, "she receives in her own big heart the bullet intended for the man she loved."

Vamp: The Rise and Fall of Theda Bara

Her co-star, Herbert Heyes, was making his film debut. He'd acted onstage with Alla Nazimova and James K. Hackett; William Fox signed him in 1916 to replace the recently departed William Shay. Like Shay, Heyes lingered under Theda's thrall in a handful of films before vanishing from the studio. He did not vanish from notice, however, boasting a long career in radio, films, and the stage until his death in 1958 (fans of the 1951 film *A Place in the Sun* will recall him as Montgomery Clift's wealthy uncle).

Under Two Flags gave Theda the chance to play an adventuress in the best sense, sort of a female Indiana Jones or Lawrence of Arabia. Galloping on horseback through the dunes of Long Island, laughing, chumming around with the soldiers in a most tomboyish way, Theda showed a whole new side to her personality. Her modest riding skills were put to the test, and she spent breaks in filming practicing (the press agents, of course, thought up all kinds of near escapes to feed the papers). Theda thoroughly enjoyed herself that month, returning exhausted each night to Manhattan.

She did, however, make time for war work. Theda was very concerned about the European war, still having family (and part of her sympathies) in Poland and France. She took two days off from filming *Under Two Flags* to attend the Allied Bazaar in Manhattan, where she spent a week's salary on charities. It was one of Theda's first shopping trips since her stardom had dawned; terrified of mobs, she usually sent a maid or Lori to shop for her. The fans at the Bazaar were enthusiastic but polite, somewhat alleviating Theda's fears.

There had only been one previous film version of *Under Two Flags* (a primitive Vitagraph short), so Theda's only competition was Blanche Bates, who had played the stage role fifteen years before. She knew she had done a great job, and she was right: *Under Two Flags* earned Theda her best reviews yet; the critics were bowled over. The reviews were unanimous raves, and all took Fox to task for not giving her more roles like Cigarette.

As Cigarette in *Under Two Flags* (1916). *Photo above: Archive Photos. Photo below: Robert S. Birchard.*

Vamp: The Rise and Fall of Theda Bara

"Miss Bara is a keen student of the camera," said W. K. Hollander of *The Chicago News*, "knows how to express herself forcibly, recognizes the screen's limitations and takes full advantage of its broad scope. She is an accomplished actress of a distinctive personality, which has been successfully directed through one channel."

All the reviews were like that: "Her superb emotional work makes Cigarette almost a work of art," "the best real acting she has done in a long time," "buoyant enthusiasm . . . vivacious personality." One sympathetic writer, suspecting what Fox had in store for the actress, said, "after the consummate art with which she has visualized Ouida's immortal daughter of the regiment . . . to go back to the stereotyped adventuress parts must be a genuine hardship for her artistic soul."

However, not everyone was totally charmed by the Long Island Sahara or by Edwards' direction. Chicago reporter Kitty Kelly wrote, "my acquaintanceship with deserts is limited, but I did not think they ran abruptly into woodlands or rivers banked by high cliffs to dive from." Kelly also provided the only negative word on Theda, who, she felt, did "somewhat overdo her kitten moments." The waste of two carloads of bran and grain — used to simulate sandstorms — also horrified a few thrifty reviewers.

But *Under Two Flags* was still a major critical success, Theda's biggest to date. For one brief shining moment, Theda Bara became a minor league Pearl White, and she loved it. White had entered films around 1910, and became one of the country's biggest stars with such adventure action serials as *The Perils of Pauline* (1914) and *The Exploits of Elaine* (1915). This is the kind of role Theda desperately wanted and rarely got to play: the plucky, wholesome all-American girl. *Under Two Flags* briefly gave her the hope that her career was taking a turn for the better.

Of course, Theda wasn't the only actress longing for a change of pace; even Lillian Gish once groused that "virgins are the hardest roles to play. Those dear little girls—to make them interesting takes great vitality, but a fallen woman or a vamp! Seventy-five percent of your work is already done."

As enthused as the critics were, *Under Two Flags* did good but not blockbuster business, and Fox Studios were barraged by letters begging for another vamp film: fans were anxious to see Theda at her worst; after all, anyone could have played Cigarette, but only Theda could be truly evil. So she was tossed next into an elaborate, torturous soap opera called *Her Double Life*.

After her great triumph as Cigarette, Theda found herself playing Mary Doone, a poor put-upon Cockney girl who is led down the path to perdition by a fiendish war correspondent (Stuart Holmes). Mary becomes a Red Cross nurse at the battle-front, takes the identity of a supposedly dead noblewoman, and returns to England to pass herself off as this girl. Amazingly, everyone buys her story (apparently Mary shed her Cockney accent along with her past). Her betrayer shows up and threatens to blow her cover (the dead noblewoman turned out to be alive) — but Mary confesses all and is accepted anyway by the warm-hearted and forgiving family, who even allow her to marry their son.

Her Double Life was far inferior to *Under Two Flags* in terms of storyline and logic. Still, Theda had won a new respect for her versatility: "The surprising Miss Bara is excellent," said John De Koven in *The Cleveland Leader*. "Her work rings with a new note of sincerity and repression." Theda Bara fans packed the theaters, and although the film got only lukewarm critical reception, it enriched the studio financially.

In the fall of 1916, Metro was preparing a version of *Romeo and Juliet*, starring married matinee idols Francis X. Bushman and Bev-

Looking rather forlorn on the set of *Her Double Life* (1916). *Photo: Lisa Bulger.*

erly Bayne. Not having learned a thing from *Carmen*, William Fox decided to film his own version of the play with Theda and Harry Hilliard in the leading roles. Hilliard — a dead ringer for Bushman — was a romantic musical comedy star who had appeared in several Broadway shows before being signed on by Fox (where he divided up his time between Theda and June Caprice). It all must have been too much for him, as Hilliard broke his contract the following year and fled the lot, never to be heard from again.

Theda, of course, was thrilled with the assignment and prattled to the press about her (probably imaginary) experiences playing Shakespeare in Europe. As usual, Fox spared no expense on sets and costumes, spending a purported $300,000. Costumes and sets outdid anything since *Carmen*: one huge interior set was built in Fort Lee, redecorated and cleverly shot forty-five different ways. The Elizabethan costumes were elaborate and realistically uncomfortable.

Fox — as always unable to let well enough alone — even improved on Shakespeare, having Juliet come briefly to life in the tomb, so she and Romeo could share a death scene. "It is a bit of a pity that Shakespeare did not think of this lively device," deadpanned one newspaper critic.

Both versions of *Romeo and Juliet* were released in October. Unlike the *Carmen* fiasco, Theda emerged the clear victor in the *Romeo and Juliet* wars. "A real triumph," was how one critic put it, and most others agreed. While many felt that Bushman out-Romeo'd Harry Hilliard, almost all agreed that Theda trounced Beverly Bayne. *Photoplay* wrote that "histrionically, Miss Bara is a better Juliet than Miss Bayne, for she brings to the play's tragic moments all the steam heat that the cool Beverly lacks." The film itself was compared to *The Birth of a Nation* by *The Louisville Post*, whose critic added that Theda "gives further and striking evidence of her ability to play almost any role, while her beauty is more evident than ever before." Another paper, obviously unfamiliar with

Theda, Walter Law, and Harry Hilliard in *Romeo and Juliet* (1916). *Photo: The Everett Collection.*

Francis X. Bushman and Beverly Bayne in the Metro version of *Romeo and Juliet. Photo: Robert S. Birchard.*

One of the impressive set pieces from *Romeo and Juliet*. *Photo: Robert S. Birchard.*

Harry Hilliard and Theda in *Romeo and Juliet*. *Photo: Robert S. Birchard.*

Vamp: The Rise and Fall of Theda Bara

Theda's frustrations, guessed that "playing the sweetly ingenuous Juliet must have irked her vampire's soul."

To play Shakespeare is the ambition of every serious actress, and to succeed is quite an accomplishment. Theda's reviews for *Romeo and Juliet* were largely favorable. Yet in retrospect, she is considered an untalented and somewhat ridiculous actress — this, despite the fact that most of her films have been unseen for more than seventy years. How did her reputation fall so far?

It must be remembered that acting styles change; Greek and Roman theater resembled Kabuki more than modern-day "acting." Performances by great Restoration actresses like Peg Woffington and Nell Gwyn would no doubt look bizarre to modern eyes. The remaining films of Sarah Bernhardt make her look like an overly enthusiastic street mime; yet no one would suggest that Bernhardt wasn't one of her era's greatest actresses.

Performers who came fresh to films fare best today: the "natural" acting of Lillian Gish and Mabel Normand, as opposed to the "stagey" acting of Alla Nazimova and Theda Bara. The fault lies not with the performer, but with their training and the expectations and proprieties of nineteenth century acting. Things moved quickly: as early as 1912, Frank Woods of *The New York Dramatic Mirror* was bemoaning, "Who can look back on the methods of picture playing three and four years ago, without a shudder?"

Theda Bara — like most of her contemporaries — was trained via the Delsarte method. François Delsarte was as influential to nineteenth-century acting as Stanislavski's "Method" was to the twentieth century. Delsarte taught specific expressions and poses to represent various moods and emotions. Very strict rules which he helped codify characterized theatrical acting: never move when another actor is speaking; only walk when you yourself are speaking; always use certain gestures with certain phrases. Acting books of the time feature specific set poses and facial expressions to indicate Joy, Coquetry, Revenge, Mirth, Fear, etc.

Not everyone followed Delsarte faithfully, of course. But even the best performers were influenced by the current conventions of stage acting. Well into the 1920's, reviews talked in Delsartian terms of performers' "registering emotion." In the early years of fan magazines, Theda and her fellow stars were pictured registering Fear, Love, Meditation, and other facial expressions. This did not indicate that they were mechanical puppets — but rather that they were up on contemporary acting styles. What they didn't know was that someone had changed the rules. Theda was still lauded during her career, but only a few years later her acting seemed laughably old fashioned. Youngsters who had never heard of Delsarte had taken over.

Fox was at a loss for film plots but didn't want to keep Theda idle that fall, so he put her in what amounted to a re-make of *The Kreutzer Sonata*, titled *The Vixen*. Once again Theda found herself playing a woman trying to break up her sister's marriage. Her character, Elsie Drummond, proclaims at one point, "it is true that I have no heart, but then I am more comfortable without one." The film was written off as "rather too heavy melodrama" by most critics, though one paper was accurate in stating that "the play will appeal to the type of audience that likes its villainy in chunks."

But it was also becoming imperative that the public know that underneath it all, Theda Bara was a really a nice, sweet-hearted thing. The 1910's were not forgiving of women who didn't follow the rules; a real-life vamp would have been run out of town on a rail. Actress Virginia Rappe is a case in point. Rappe is best known for dying under mysterious circumstances at a 1921 party in San

"He's dead!"

Above, below and lower right: Theda "registers emotions" for *Motion Picture Magazine. Photos: Chester Clarke.*

"Don't strike!"   "He loves another!"

Theda in the dressing room Fox built for her in his West Coast studio. *Photo: The Everett Collection.*

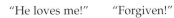

"He loves me!"   "Forgiven!"

Vamp: The Rise and Fall of Theda Bara

As home-wrecking Elsie Drummond in *The Vixen* (1916). *Photo: Wisconsin Center for Film and Theater Research.*

Francisco. Comic Roscoe "Fatty" Arbuckle was accused and finally acquitted of her death. But Rappe herself became the object of condemnation when it was discovered she was not a virgin and had undergone several abortions. Rappe — an illegitimate girl from a poverty-stricken background — was written off by Hollywood as a tramp who simply got what she deserved. Women had to be careful of their reputations as late as 1950, when Ingrid Bergman was run out of Hollywood for having a baby out of wedlock. Fox began making sure that everyone was quite aware that his prize vamp was an Edwardian Valentine underneath her makeup.

Theda seems to have gone overboard during one interview — in trying to be sweet and girlish, she instead sounded as though she'd entirely lost her mind. "I look at my canary," Theda twittered to an astonished Delight Evans, "and I say, `Dicky, am I so wicked?' And Dicky says, `Tweet, tweet.' That may mean `yes, yes,' or `no, no,' may it not?"

There was also a strain of feminism in Theda's publicity. One of the more interesting quotes the Fox publicity department put into Theda's mouth came early in her career. "Believe me, for every woman vampire there are ten men of the same type," Theda was quoted in May of 1915. "Men who take everything from women — love, devotion, beauty, youth and give nothing in return! V stands for Vampire and it stands for Vengeance, too. The vampire that I play is the vengeance of my sex upon its exploiters. You see, I have the face of a vampire, perhaps, but the heart of a `feministe.'"

For decades this quote has been used by writers claiming Theda as a women's rights activist. Even in the extremely unlikely case that the words are Theda's own, they display the worst of men's fears about feminists: vengeful, castrating harpies bent on punishing men for their misdeeds. The resurgence of the equal rights movement in the 1910's and the suffragettes of both England and the U.S. terrified men and some women as well. Theda's public image reaffirmed these people's notions that such women, given an inch, would turn to the bad.

Theda Bara herself was a true daughter of the nineteenth century, who later gave up her career to keep her husband happy. When cornered by a reporter who asked her about "The Suffrage Question" in 1917, Theda hemmed and hawed, not eager to offend her studio or her audience. "I have very great doubts as to the wisdom of universal suffrage by amendment to the constitution," she said, "but I have never studied the subject as thoroughly as it deserves and therefore am a bit reluctant to positively commit myself." Trying to back herself out of a corner, she went on. "I do not question the fact that women are as capable as men in doing a great many things but whether they can exercise the same degree of wisdom in casting the ballot is to be determined." After endorsing President Wilson's suggestion that the question be decided state by state, she gratefully went back to plugging her latest film. Although an independent working woman, Theda Bara was not Susan B. Anthony.

Some of her audience, however, did see a strong woman and loved it — few would want to act like the characters Theda played, but they got a thrill out of watching her cut a swath through the male of the species. One of Theda's fans, Felicia Blake, even wrote an angry feminist answer to Rudyard Kipling's famous poem:

> A Fool there was and she lowered her pride
> (Even as you and I.)
> To a bunch of conceit in a masculine hide —
> We saw the faults that could not be denied,
> But the fool saw only his manly side
> (Even as you and I.)
>
> Oh, the love she laid on her own heart's grave
> With the care of her head and hand,
> Belongs to the man who did not know,
> (And now she knows that he never could know)
> And did not understand.
>
> A Fool there was, and her best she gave,
> (Even as you and I.)
> Of noble thoughts, of gay and grave,
> (And all were accepted as due to the knave,)
> But the fool would never her folly save
> (Even as you and I.)

Oh, the stabs she hid, which the Lord forbid
Had ever been really planned,
She took from the man who didn't know why
(And now she knows that he never knew why)
And did not understand.

The fool was loved while the game was new
(Even as you and I.)
And when it was played, she took her cue,
(Plodding along as most of us do,)
Trying to keep his faults from view,
(Even as you and I.)

And it isn't the ache of the heart, or its break,
That stings like a white hot brand—
It's the learning to know that she raised a god,
And bent her head to kiss the rod,
For the one who could not understand.

The film Theda was trying to promote when sidelined by the Suffrage Question was *The Darling of Paris*, filmed late in 1916 and released in January of the following year. Very loosely based on Victor Hugo's novel *Notre Dame de Paris* (better known as *The Hunchback of Notre Dame*), this film is a good example of how fast and loose some companies played with their source material. It was decided to change the evil priest character into an evil scientist, so as not to offend the clergy. It was also decided to *cure* Quasimodo of his hunchback, as who wants to look at a hunchbacked hero? The bulk of the film's plot fell to Theda's role, the gypsy dancing girl Esmeralda, but she still needed a clean-cut handsome love interest.

Vamp: The Rise and Fall of Theda Bara

The plot of *The Darling of Paris* will baffle anyone familiar with Lon Chaney's or Charles Laughton's hunchbacks of Notre Dame. The wealthy Esmeralda is kidnapped by gypsies at birth and becomes, as one might assume, the darling of Paris. She is loved by Quasimodo (the bell ringer and former hunchback), Frallo (the wicked surgeon who cured him), and an equally wicked Captain. The surgeon kills the Captain and frames Esmeralda, but after many merry mix-ups, she winds back with her wealthy family, happily wed to Quasimodo.

The Darling of Paris was yet another hit for Theda, her fifth moneymaker in a row. Amazingly, not many critics objected to the mangling of Hugo's tale. "The wisdom of these changes is without question, if the commercial returns from the picture are to decide the matter," shrugged *Motion Picture World*, while another paper called the film "thrilling and sensational." The expensive Parisian settings (constructed in Fort Lee, as usual) and the reproduction of Notre Dame Cathedral got raves, as did Theda herself. "It is a fitting role for the gifts of the talented actress," said *The Chicago Post*.

Even the censors loved her for a change; there was very little in this film for them to leave on the cutting room floor. It was headline-worthy news when The National Board of Review passed *The Darling of Paris* uncut and with "Excellent" stamped on it.

Theda was especially lauded for her characterization of the wild peasant girl; she managed to make Esmeralda both crude and sympathetic with only a week or two of preparation. Moving picture directors in the 1910's rarely gave their players the chance to think out or develop their characters — indeed, extended rehearsals were the exception rather than the rule. Even the much-lauded D. W. Griffith directed his performers in an off-hand way that would horrify modern actors. "You didn't usually have time for characterizations in pictures in those days," said Griffith actress Blanche Sweet, "because you got through as quickly as you could

Cuddling with Betsy the goat on the set of *The Darling of Paris* (1917). *Photo: Archive Photos.*

do it adequately. I mean, you did the best you could, but you couldn't take time."

Mae Marsh — one of Griffith's finest actresses — described his directing style, typical of the day. "He explained, `I want you to sit on that rock wall over there. This boy you're sitting next to, you're very, very much in love with him. Have you ever been in love?' And I said, oh yes, which I hadn't. He said, `just think that you're terribly in love and look up at him shy-like.' So I did, and then he said, `look up at him again and then put your head down,' which I did. Then he said, `now, get up and run away.' So I got up and ran away. . . . I said to Mr. Griffith, when am I going to do it again? He said, `you've done it once. You can't do it again. That was fine. Maybe you can do something else tomorrow.'"

Fox was not Biograph, and none of their directors were D. W. Griffith, so Theda had to put up with treatment considerably more terse than did Sweet or Marsh. It has always been considered polite to sit and feed actors lines when they are filming close-ups — none of that nonsense went on at Fox. Theda would "register emotion" to an imaginary co-star, who would be off filming scenes with the second-unit director. One reporter, impressed by this time-saving scheme, marvelled, "such is the efficiency of the Fox plant; and Mr. Edwards, Theda Bara's director, is deserving of some praise, manipulating the scenes in order to use every minute of the players' time whenever it is possible . . . The Fox plant must be the place where efficiency was originated."

This hurry-up work style added to the siege mentality of the stock company, and Theda — who was in nearly every scene of her films — was on constant duty from the time she arrived to the time she crawled home to bed. Her few free minutes were spent repairing her make-up, changing costumes, or acting for reporters on the set.

In late 1916, Selig and Goldfrap — having finally abandoned Theda's Arabian birth tale — came up with another successful story. Theda's contract was coming up for renewal in May of 1917 and negotiations were already under way. This gave the PR men an idea: they released a story to the press that Theda had renegotiated her contract, "one of the strangest contracts ever entered into between star and manager." The stipulations in this supposed three-year agreement stated that Theda:

- Must not marry;
- Must not appear in public without veils;
- Must not ride in public transportation;
- Must not take her "constitutional" during daylight;
- Must have curtains put over her car windows so as not to be seen;
- Must not go to Turkish Baths ("of which she is very fond," one newspaper assured us);
- Must not allow private snapshots to be taken of herself.

The contract, of course, never existed; it was another of Selig and Goldfrap's wild inventions. And a good one, too — it got plenty of newsprint and was repeated as gospel truth for decades. Contracts and money *were* on Theda's mind, however; she was assessed for $20,000 in back taxes (the fine was later reduced to $5,400).

Yet another press release that month noted that 162 babies had been named for Theda, "and all white!" Though their racial makeup cannot be vouched for, the release is accurate in one sense: it's not at all unusual to run into elderly Theda babies of 1910's vintage (one wound up working at Tiffany's in New York).

Theda was back to vamping with a vengeance in *The Tiger Woman*; her Princess Petrovitch was one of the most unapologetically evil characters she ever played. The Princess — in only six reels — managed to rob her husband, poison her lover, and force another lover to kill his father, all the while wearing expensive Poirot gowns. She is finally done in by a blackmailing servant. As one bemused reviewer put it, "the wholesale damage that strews her pathway would put a Kansas cyclone to shame." *The Tiger Woman* was one of those films which critics hated and audiences loved: fans shrieked with delight as Theda wrought her wicked work, throwing herself into the role with admirable enthusiasm.

Probably Theda's most hilarious hat, from *The Tiger Woman* (1917). *Photo: Jerry Ohlinger.*

Most reviews, however, were like this one: "Theda runs the gamut of badness and sends the spectators away rejoicing. Personally, I have no use for a photoplay of this kind."

A lot of people did, though: in January 1917, *Motion Picture* magazine's poetic New Year's "gift" to Theda read,

Theda Bara do not pause,
For Vampires we adore;
And may the New Year give you cause
To Vampire more and more!

Come spring, Theda found herself back in St. Augustine for
what was becoming a yearly trip; *Her Greatest Love* and *Heart and
Soul* were shot practically in tandem that season. She was already
something of a local legend in St. Augustine; during this trip, General Foster of the Chamber of Commerce invited her to a tree-
planting ceremony, where Theda labored with spade and shovel
for the newspaper photographers, planting her very own honorary
tree. She was even persuaded to appear in person at a Jacksonville
theater showing *The Tiger Woman*, where fifteen thousand
screaming fans besieged her for autographs.

She also managed to get away from the crowds, using breaks
from filming to trot around on her mount, Teddy, among the sand
dunes. Taking full advantage of this, Selig and Goldfrap released a
story that Theda had "fallen off her horse near a dangerous five-
hundred-year-old alligator."

Her two Florida location films opened in the spring of 1917,
but their reception did little to assure Theda about her future.
She'd played two good girls — roles that could have been written
for Mary Pickford — and both films flopped resoundingly.

Her Greatest Love was, perhaps, her worst film, and by all
accounts, contained her worst performance. Theda played Vera
Herbert, an angelic young girl forced by her wicked family into
marriage with a dissolute Russian Prince. Dressed in pinafores and
curls, Theda unaccountably kept her vampire makeup on and
overacted abominably. The fact that the U. S. entered World War I

With Alice Gale in the dreadful *Her Greatest Love* (1917). *Photo: Archive Photos.*

Her Greatest Love. Photo: Robert S. Birchard.

the week *Her Greatest Love* opened certainly didn't help pack the theaters. Additionally, critics were not kind. One reviewer developed into a regular Theda-basher. The syndicated Mae Tinee (a pseudonym — evidently a lame pun on "Matinee") let Theda have it with both barrels: "Taking it as burlesque, I may say that as an unintentional comedienne I think Miss Bara has Charlie Chaplin backed off the boards. If you ever in your life saw anything funnier than Theda Bara thus garbed rolling around her beblackened eyes in horror at the sight of her harridanlike mother lighting a cigarette, I miss my guess."

Most of the reviews were like that: Louella Parsons wrote that "had I a heart less kind I could fill many pages telling why Miss

Bara should never be cast as a young girl, unsophisticated and innocent." And if Theda pinned any hopes on *Heart and Soul*, she was soon disappointed. When that film opened a month after *Her Greatest Love* fled town, it was almost as big a disaster.

Heart and Soul was based on *Jess*, one of Rider Haggard's western novels. Taking advantage of the Florida locale, J. Gordon Edwards elected to set the film in Hawaii (though some reviews have the film taking place in Puerto Rico or Cuba). It was an expensive shoot: a huge plantation was built (with ten thousand sugar canes stuck into the ground) and then burned for the film. Theda portrayed a sweet girl who sacrifices herself for her sister's happiness, even giving up her life so her sister and new brother-in-law may escape an insurrection.

Reviews were only slightly more kind than they'd been for *Her Greatest Love*. Even those critics who felt Theda did well in the part carped that "I like her better with fascinating negligees swirling about her, heavily tinted fingernails and a cigarette between her lips." *The Cleveland Leader* cried, "may she soon be re-vamped!"

Fox read these reviews, of course, and more importantly looked over the sorry box office receipts for *Her Greatest Love* and *Heart and Soul*. They were to be Theda's last non-vampire roles for a long time.

But two of her biggest successes were just around the corner.

On returning to New York, Theda bided her time while her next big film was being prepared. She appeared at a benefit at Brooklyn's Academy of Music for firemen who'd been injured in the line of duty. Her carefully rehearsed speech delighted the attendees: "If, when I die," Theda said from her box seat, "I should be found guilty of all those actions I have depicted on the screen and

the Philippines in 1903, then barnstormed with stock companies through the south and west. Roscoe formed his own stock company, then hit Broadway in 1915, entering films that same year. A publicity man's dream, he'd also been — or so he claimed — a Mountie in Canada and a cowboy in Montana. Tall, dark and handsome, he really looked the part of Armand Duvall.

The story was surefire, based on an actual tragedy and written with passion and wit by Alexandre Dumas. His grisly 1848 novel was adapted into a considerably romanticized play in 1852; two years later Verdi based his opera *La Traviata* on the play. *Camille* was the story of a good-hearted but flighty country girl who becomes a successful prostitute in Paris, winning the heart of a respectable young man before dying of tuberculosis. Dumas based the tale on a woman he himself had loved, Alphonsine Plessis (renamed Marguerite Gautier in the novel), who was only in her 20's when she died in 1847.

The role was an actress' dream: Bernhardt, Olga Nethersole, Nance O'Neil, Eleanora Duse, Margaret Anglin, Eva Le Gallienne, and Lillian Gish all brought Marguerite to Broadway. *Camille* had already been filmed by Bernhardt in 1912 and Clara Kimball Young in 1915 (later, Norma Talmadge, Marie Prevost and Greta Garbo brought her to the screen as well). Theda was in good company and very excited about the role. As usual, she ran to the library to read the book and play and consulted with period experts about Paris of the 1840's. She was somewhat disconcerted when she discovered her Marguerite was to be of 1917 vintage.

If she had to play another vamp, Marguerite Gautier was an acceptable compromise for Theda. She threw herself into her role (as did Alice Gale who, as Prudence, got rave reviews). The film didn't open till late September, giving the country a whole summer off from Theda, long enough for the taste of her last two films to vanish. The late autumn opening was also due to the summer heat and to censors who tore into *Camille* with gusto. When the film finally opened, though, audiences were delighted to see Theda back at the old stand, vamping away.

Both Theda and J. Gordon Edwards were praised for their efforts, and crowds once again poured into theaters. One of the few nay-sayers was a critic who loved Theda but hated the play, "that immortal concoction of driveling sentimentality . . . Personally, we prefer it on the screen because we don't have to listen to the coughing." While most felt that "Miss Bara makes Camille the brazen hussy we believe she was," one or two noted that the healthy Theda — weighing in at something over 130 pounds — was less than convincing as a consumptive. It took a big, husky Armand to lift her onto her deathbed in the final reel.

Between films — between shots — Theda sat for her photo. Since so many of Theda's films no longer exist, she is largely remembered through these stills. This is a special shame, as the art of Hollywood photography was still in its infancy in the 1910's — Theda never sat for George Hurrell, Ruth Harriet Louise, or Eugene Robert Richee, like the stars of the 1920's and 1930's.

For her formal portrait stills, Theda went to studios like Underwood and Underwood or Sarony in New York, who produced some truly lovely work. One photographer — who simply signed himself "Mishkin," took some of Theda's most striking early vamp poses, hair flowing wildly, draped in black robes. When Theda moved west, Fox hired talented freelance photographer F. A. Witzel to take most of her stills, but many more were taken by now-anonymous staffers.

Theda had to spend many of her non-working hours venturing to the fast-proliferating Los Angeles portrait studios, as it wasn't until the 1920's that film companies built their own in-house sitting rooms. Fortunately, Theda loved the still camera. Not terribly photogenic, she studied her best angles and lighting, and quickly learned not to smile for the lens — she looked best either in profile or straight-on, deadpan, and carefully lit. Sadly, the heavy make-up required to publicize her vamp roles was unflattering; her few photos with light make-up are startling and show an entirely different woman.

On-the-set stills had to be taken for press handouts, newspaper reviews, and theater displays. After a scene was shot, one of Fox's anonymous still men would corral Theda and her co-stars into striking artistic poses. Whether or not these poses bore any connection to the plot was unimportant (a rule which still stands today). As long as it looked good, who cared?

As many as twenty shots were taken for each set and costume. Many of these were donated by Lori Bara to Lincoln Center's Performing Arts Collection; Theda and her co-stars can be seen trying every pose they could think of. While shooting *Sin*, Theda and William Shay were placed in front of a huge altar, hitting pose after pose after pose: Theda flinches from Shay; he flinches from her. She steals the jewel; he steals the jewel. She kneels at his feet, then he at hers. In one still, the two (obviously tired by this time) simply break up laughing, gesturing helplessly towards the photographer.

Obviously, these stills don't give any indication of acting skill. They show off the sets and costumes beautifully, but the tired and uninspired actors often mug shamelessly or sit glumly. However, these photos are the only record left with which books (this one included) can represent now-lost films.

In the spring of 1917, Theda was handed her biggest assignment: her next film was to become her most famous, but would also uproot her from the city and home she loved.

Portrait still, late 1910's. *Photo: Arbe Bareis.*

Chapter 6

The Girl of the Golden West

Theda was at the very height of her fame in mid-1917; she was fully as big a star as Chaplin, Pickford, or Fairbanks. Fox chose this time to star her in what would become her most successful — and famous — film. It seemed an obvious role for her. Fans and reviewers had been hinting for more than a year that they'd like to see Theda as The Queen of the Nile, and Fox had been planning *Cleopatra* as early as the end of 1915. The film was shot during the summer of 1917 and released late in October.

Cleopatra, who ruled Egypt for twenty-one years before her death in 30 B. C. at the age of thirty-nine, proved irresistible to playwrights and, later, to film makers. Theda Bara was not the screen's first Cleopatra, not by a long shot. The first known version was filmed by Georges Méliès in 1899. *Cleopatra* was filmed again in 1908 and as Vitagraph's *Cleopatra's Lover* in 1909, but the first big-budget production was producer/writer/star Helen Gardner's 1911 *Cleopatra* (which, unlike Theda's, still exists).

Fox wanted to film a *Cleopatra* to end all *Cleopatra*s. He imported two impressive co-stars: Fritz Leiber, a noted Shakespearean actor, played Julius Caesar, and Thurston Hall, who had appeared on Broadway in *Ben-Hur*, was Marc Antony. Both men were well into middle age, but talent and reputation rather than sex appeal recommended them. Both continued acting till their deaths, Hall appearing on the TV series *Topper* in the 1950's.

As enthusiastic as Theda was about the film, there was no getting away from the one big drawback: she would finally have to move to California. For more than a year she'd been able to convince Fox that sets and locations could be just as easily be filmed in

Vamp: The Rise and Fall of Theda Bara

New York, New Jersey or Florida. But the huge pyramids, Sphinx, and splendors of ancient Rome and Egypt simply could not be faked on the East Coast. The film industry was slowly running west like sand in an hourglass, and Theda, unwillingly, would have to go with the flow. She saw less and less of William Fox, who stayed at his 50th Street headquarters in Manhattan. From now on, orders would be filtered through Winfield Sheehan, promoted to Fox's West Coast General Manager.

Not everyone felt about California as Theda did. Agnes DeMille moved to Hollywood with her father William around the same time, and raved to Kevin Brownlow in the late 1970's about the abundance of flowers, "all of them exquisite, all of them blooming wild in the open fields." Actress Leatrice Joy spoke of bands of poppies lining the railroad tracks heading west. "It was just like heaven with two beautiful welcome arms, just saying `come to California.' And of course in my romantic way I responded, I was so grateful I was getting out to California where they *really* made pictures."

Theda begged to differ. New York had museums, libraries, higher-class clothing and book stores. It had nineteenth (and still some eighteenth) century architecture. It had culture and history — California had little of this, and the intellectual snob in Theda rebelled.

Before leaving New York, Theda took advantage of one of the city's cultural landmarks. She contacted Mr. Lithgow, curator of the Egyptian collection at the Metropolitan Museum of Art, and crammed as much Egyptian costume and architectural history into her notebook as possible. Theda later noted proudly that "liberties were taken with the story, but *not* with the settings." She said that the Queen of the Nile was actually a hardworking mother and politician, but that Fox felt a fiery vampire would make for better business.

Theda (accompanied by her mother, Lori, and a handful of servants) left from Grand Central Station early in May, as more than a thousand fans crowded around for a glimpse of her, tossing flowers and snapping photos.

The train trip west took several weeks as Theda made stops along the way. In Chicago, she fled the heat to a cool dark suite at the Hotel Blackstone, where Selig and Goldfrap arranged for her to meet the local press. Her conversation with *The Chicago News'* W. K. Hollander was unusually candid; Hollander found that Theda "made her hearers forget the vampire of the screen during her dissertation." When asked if she preferred vampire roles, Theda said somewhat wearily, "it isn't a matter of preference. The theatergoers want it and their wishes must be gratified. I have departed from these parts in one or more pictures and instantly I received hundreds of letters asking me to return to them."

Hollander noted that Theda seemed somewhat impatient at stupid or impertinent questions (such as enquiring if she received hate mail, which she most certainly did not). But she also professed herself happy with her work. "I have my inspirational moments, and sense when I am doing my best. No matter how extravagantly I am praised after a scene is taken at the studio, if the bell within me fails to ring, I am not satisfied that I have achieved good results."

Theda finally arrived in Los Angeles in late May 1917, moving right into a large faux-Tudor home at 649 West Adams Boulevard, a then-fashionable section of West Los Angeles. William Fox had furnished the place in Early Vampire. According to actress Leatrice Joy, who later became a friend, the house was heavy with ottomans, fur rugs and beaded curtains. "The walls were hung with cretonne prints and the air reeked of a heavy musk," Joy told her daughter. "There was a caged snake on a shelf, which Theda would stroke in the presence of the press but which slept and ate bugs at all other times."

Vamp: The Rise and Fall of Theda Bara

Theda's West Adams Boulevard house. *Photo: New York Public Library for the Performing Arts.*

West Adams Boulevard was a rather stuffy neighborhood, and residents were not thrilled to see an actress — certainly not *that* actress! — move in, trailed by fans and reporters. At least one neighbor was happy to see her, however. Leatrice Joy, although she'd not yet met Theda, came knocking at her door for dating advice. Believing Theda's publicity (even though Joy herself was an actress), she felt the famed vampire could help her seduce her then-boyfriend, later-husband, John Gilbert. Theda happily took Joy off to her dressing room and made her up as a Baby Vampire. Puffing some rouge on Joy's earlobes, Theda gave one of her well-known Theda Bara impersonations: "Zis is for earlobes pulsing vit ze blood of love," she purred. "Zis means passion."

Joy's horrified mother scrubbed her daughter clean before the date in question, but missed the earlobes. When John Gilbert asked Joy if she were getting an ear infection, she laughed, "that's my seething passion!"

Theda settled somewhat uncomfortably into her new abode,

though she preferred the light and airy bungalow dressing-room Fox prepared on the lot for her.

Well before the release, or even shooting, of *Cleopatra*, the publicity department began gearing up for what would become the biggest — and silliest — promotion of the era. As early as April, Selig and Goldfrap released a statement to the press about an inscription found "on a stone wall in a tomb near Thebes," forecasting the coming of Theda Bara. The 2,500-year-old prophecy read,

> I, Rhames, priest of Set, tell you this: She shall seem a snake to most men; she shall lead them to sin, and to their destruction. Yet she shall not be so. She shall be good and virtuous, and kind of heart; but she shall not seem so to most men. For she shall not be that which she appears. She shall be called . . .

After which the Greek letter "Theta" appeared. It seemed that not only was Rhames a priest of Set, but a Theda Bara fan as well, as he managed to fit the titles of two of her films (*Sin* and *Destruction*) into his prediction. According to unnamed scientists and language students, the letters "t" and "d" were interchangeable in ancient Greece, thereby excusing Rhames for misspelling Theda's name.

Theda also received from an anonymous source "a beautifully illumined card with strange Egyptian hieroglyphics," which she — suddenly an Egyptian linguist — translated as a tribute from one of Cleopatra's recently reincarnated servants. Theda played up her press conferences and interviews for all they were worth. At one point she declared herself the reborn spirit of a daughter of Seti, high priest of the Pharaohs, and was photographed at a museum gazing soulfully into the coffin of what she claimed was her own mummy.

Vamp: The Rise and Fall of Theda Bara

Cleopatra (1917) *Photo: Robert S. Birchard.*

Of course, it didn't take Theda long to decide that she had actually been Cleopatra herself in an earlier life. She acted "spookier" than ever, according to Archie Bell, who had long been accustomed to her high jinks. Now Theda took to choking down raw beef and lettuce for lunch, not eating till her statuette of Amen-Ra was safely sitting by her plate. Gazing into her ice water as though it were a crystal, Theda told dreamily of her former life as Queen of the Nile and flashed a 2,000-year-old ring given to her by a 110-year-old sheik.

"I felt the blood of the Ptolemys coursing through my veins," she emoted. "I know that I am a reincarnation of Cleopatra. It is not a mere theory in my mind. I have positive knowledge that such is the case. I live Cleopatra, I breathe Cleopatra, I *am* Cleopatra!"

"I lived in ancient Egypt," she continued, "probably at Thebes.

Fox's rather alarming vision of the Sphinx's original appearance. *Photo: Robert S. Birchard.*

I remember crossing the Nile on barges to Karnak and Luxor as plainly as I recall crossing the Hudson on the ferry . . ." Years later Theda laughed, "I was never any nearer Egypt than an Egyptian cigarette!"

Fan magazines and newspapers thought all this was hilarious and printed it with tongue in cheek. No longer taken in by Fox publicity, they either played along or kidded it with deadpan articles about Theda's latest incarnation. The public wasn't fooled either, but everyone thought it was such great harmless fun that no one objected.

It was at this point that someone at Fox — never named, but one hopes he or she got a bonus — discovered that Theda Bara's name was an anagram for "Arab Death." Selig and Goldfrap practically fell all over themselves playing that up (it was such a good

The uncomfortable star tries to avoid sunburn while filming *Cleopatra*.

J. Gordon Edwards directs Theda and her Antony (Thurston Hall). *Photos: Robert S. Birchard.*

Theda with her puppy "Admiral Peary."

Theda adjusts her headgear while J. Gordon Edwards directs some Romans.
Photos: Robert S. Birchard.

gag that many later writers assumed Theda's stage name had been invented for just that reason).

Meanwhile, of course, filming continued apace (Theda bought a home movie camera to record her adventures on the set — sadly, these too have been lost). Fox reportedly spent $500,000 on the sets, which included hundreds of rugs, tapestries and hangings. In the bean fields of Ventura County, the pyramids and the Sphinx were reproduced. (In 1917, the Sphinx still had not been completely excavated, so Theda's version was missing its paws.) In Balboa, a fleet of warships was constructed for a huge battle scene; outside Venice (California, that is), canals and the Alexandria waterfront were raised. Los Angeles sets were used for temples and the Roman Forum. Thirty thousand people were supposedly employed on the film: actors, extras, carpenters, costumers and crew, as well as two thousand horses.

The most difficult scene to film was the battle of Actium, shot in Balboa. One local schoolgirl recalled that scores of townspeople were hired as galley slaves and soldiers, and that filming became a town festival for weeks. Miraculously, no one was seriously injured, as hundreds of amateur soldiers whaled away at each other and armor-clad sailors toppled off their galleys into the water.

J. Gordon Edwards had his hands full: with hundreds of extras on hand in the broiling sun, he had to shoot between exercises being carried out by the U. S. Aviation Training Camp at Ventura. No sooner would he start shooting than a dozen or so airplanes would appear over the Roman fleet, ruining the take.

A local historian wrote that "the climax to weeks of filming came one fine night when the fleet was burned. Great torches were lighted to illuminate the scene. We sat for hours on the bank above the lakes until the rehearsal was over and the ships were burning and the galley slaves were screaming and jumping into the water."

Theda wasn't particularly surprised by the script, which favored Cleopatra's supposedly passionate love affairs with Marc Antony and Julius Caesar over her wily political skills. After all, she'd been at Fox long enough to know what gets an audience into a theater. But she was quite taken aback when presented with her costumes, or lack of same.

The costumes worn by Theda in *Cleopatra* bear a startling resemblance to those adorning Madonna in her racier videos. The most famous is the snake-bra: Theda was decked out in long dangling earrings, snake-like headband, a few strips of brocade for a skirt, and a halter-top consisting of two intertwined snakes with rather impolite rubies serving for eyes. Theda's breasts and upper thighs were all but exposed throughout the film: her imaginative brassieres (painfully applied with spirit gum) included flowered pasties and what appeared to be rhinestone-covered pancakes.

Despite her horror at this display, Theda threw herself into the role with great enthusiasm (according to some critics, a little too much enthusiasm). Her penchant for realism in fight scenes was noted by one on-the-set reporter. At one point in the film, Cleopatra had to rough up the messenger bringing bad tidings. During rehearsal, Theda was heard to order the cowering actor (Hector Sarno), "now, don't run away before I beat you this time!"

Reporter Kenneth Beaton visited the set on a day when Theda and Thurston Hall were shooting a particularly passionate love scene. "He had her in his arms crying for air, and they came up and breathed deeply, and went down again," Beaton observed. "And the director said, `that's all right.' And they broke and Antony went over and sat on the running board of a Ford and lighted his pipe." Beaton strolled over to ask Theda if she enjoyed her work;

Sadly, the designer of these remarkable costumes is unknown. *Photos: above left, Archive Photos; others, Robert S. Birchard.*

Cleopatra vamps her Caesar (Fritz Leiber). This scene was censored in several states. *Photo: Robert S. Birchard.*

she smiled wearily and asked him if he enjoyed *his*, before going off to fix her makeup.

Much to everyone's surprise, both The National Board of Review and the usually tough Ohio Board of Censors passed the film with no cuts. Mrs. Miller, Ohio's head censor, explained that "the producers have followed history in a remarkable way, and Miss Bara's interpretation of the character is so skillfully and convincingly done that I feel justified in passing the picture as it was brought to the censor offices."

Major Funkhouser of Chicago felt no such need and made major cuts in *Cleopatra*, stating that Theda wore entirely too little in the way of costumes. Theda — via Fox, of course — sued Funkhouser for $100,000, claiming defamation of character. "That was a company matter," Theda told a reporter. "Really I would rather not discuss it." Changing her mind, she went on furiously:

Left: Theda's snakes hold on for dear life. *Photo: Arbe Bareis. Right:* The death of the Queen. *Photo: Robert S. Birchard.*

"[Major Funkhouser] doesn't know the least thing about art. If he did he would have appreciated the production. It was historical and the heroine was one of the foremost women of ancient history." The suit, if it ever really existed, was eventually dropped.

Fox opened the film with a bang in Los Angeles on October 14, accompanying the showing with a full orchestra and specially written score. Theda herself appeared at the première in Clune's Auditorium, visibly sinking further and further into her seat as she became "bara and bara" on-screen. She was cheered and pelted with flowers at the end of the film.

From beginning to end, *Cleopatra* must have been a remarkable film. It is one of the most sought-after of the missing silent classics today. The immense sets, bizarre costumes, and what appears to have been some ace direction and camera work made it a special treat. The opening scene, for example, consisted of an amazing

139

J. Gordon Edwards and Theda Bara in front of her dressing room on the Fox lot in California. *Photo: Robert S. Birchard.*

dolly shot. The film began with a long view of the desert, the pyramids, and the Sphinx. Slowly, then faster, the camera raced forwards, closer and closer to the Sphinx. As the camera neared the statue's face, it dissolved into the image of Cleopatra, her eyes suddenly opening.

Fox's booking agent, Samuel Kingston, sent out road shows nationwide, with ticket prices of a dollar; orchestras accompanied the film in most large cities. Crowds jammed theaters and most had turn-away business for *Cleopatra's* entire run. Box-office records were broken in New York, Washington, D.C., Buffalo and Schenectady, and many theaters dropped their planned schedules to book return engagements. *The New York Telegraph* reported that all segments of the population were bitten by Bara-itis. "In Washington the most fashionable people of the city attended and the

Theda studying a script on the porch. *Photo: Robert S. Birchard.*

business increased each day until toward the end of the week it was impossible to obtain seats. In Schenectady it played to the industrial classes and both days were `sell-outs'."

No copies of *Cleopatra* are known to exist, though some may still lie moldering in a film vault or attic. It is impossible to judge the film today, as reviews were evenly divided: half felt that *Cleopatra* was the equal of *Intolerance* and that Theda gave the greatest performance of the year. The rest felt the film was garbage and Theda an overstuffed ham.

Theda saved all of her reviews, good and bad. "Theda Bara is excellent," said *Motion Picture Magazine*, "and does some of the best work of her career." The *Los Angeles Times* wrote that "Theda Bara has again scored one of the splendid triumphs of her conquering career." The well-regarded *Photoplay* felt that "Miss Bara rises to heights of tragic expression hitherto unsuspected, not by ravings or hysteria, but by the sheer grace of despair." *The Boston Post* praised "the brilliant work of Theda Bara, who grasped the subtleties of the character in a most wonderful way." "Theda Bara is a surprise and a revelation," wrote a Spokane reviewer, adding that the film was "one of the most gorgeous spectacles Spokane has seen for a long time" (this was presumably meant as a compliment).

These reviews are quoted at length to show the enormous dichotomy between opinions. It's hard to believe that the following critics saw the same movie: "Caesar and Cleopatra," carped *The Cleveland Press*, "are posturing and raving even when they are alone, and pose as stiffly as a citizen in a boiled shirt before the camera of a village photographer." Another critic claimed that Theda "rolls her eyes and her hips in that manner which the circus side-show has taught us is thoroughly Egyptian." Calling the entire film a "burlesque," *The Brooklyn Eagle* felt that Theda's Cleopatra "could never tempt a man to be late for dinner, much less to give up the throne of Rome. When she was not repulsive, she was funny."

One of the things that makes it so difficult to assess Theda Bara as an actress — in the absence of most of her work — is that reviewers either loved her or hated her; she was like olives and Elvis. *The Brooklyn Eagle* referred to Theda as "one of the worst actresses now appearing on any stage," while *The New Jersey Telegraph* called her "one of the best motion picture actresses in the country." However reviewers might feel, though, her fans were rabid in her defense, and every bad notice brought an onslaught of furious letters. One fan wrote to his local paper, "why in your theater articles do you always knock Theda Bara? You said she was too old as Esmeralda . . . " to which the critic replied, "We did not say Miss Bara was `old' as Esmeralda. `Coarse and clumsy' were the adjectives employed in that review."

6 / The Girl of the Golden West

More than a few reviews indelicately brought up Theda's figure, which was generously displayed throughout *Cleopatra*. Theda, who stood 5'6", claimed her weight was 132 pounds throughout her career, a forgivable understatement. When Joe Williams of *The Cleveland Leader* called her plump, scores of furious letters poured into his office — including one from Theda herself. This prompted a follow-up column, an open letter to the actress. "You struck me as exceedingly well fed," Williams responded, after complimenting her acting, and maintaining that "the screen enthusiast doesn't care a resonant rap whether his favorite resembles a corn-fed chicken or a railroad sandwich."

Others were concerned with Theda's body as well — not its poundage, but the percentage on view. The Better Film Committee of the Women's Club of Omaha condemned *Cleopatra*, Mrs. Benjamin Baker stating, "I never let the thought out of my mind that she was a pagan, not a Christian woman . . . but I must confess to being shocked at the movements and few clothes worn by the actress. She certainly was Hooverizing* on clothes." Commenting on the Women's Club decision, Winfield Sheehan condescendingly stated, "If the women condemn a picture, they are right. The women are always right," he continued, beaming paternally. "It makes no difference to me what they do or say, they are right."Other papers were delighted with Theda's lack of cover: "If Cleopatra didn't look like Theda Bara her contemporaries were the losers, and if she didn't dress like her then she failed to take advantage of a warm and pleasant climate." Another paper cracked, "How does Theda Bara compare to other Cleopatras? She outstrips 'em all!"

Love it or hate it, *Cleopatra* was the biggest hit of 1917, easily overwhelming such worthy box office opponents as Mary Pickford's *Rebecca of Sunnybrook Farm*, Alice Joyce's melodrama *Within*

*In 1917, President Wilson appointed Herbert Hoover as Chairman of the Food Administration Board; Hoover encouraged economy and conservation.

Cleopatra. Photo: Robert S. Birchard.

the Law, Irene Castle's adventure serial *Patria* and such Chaplin shorts as *Easy Street* and *The Immigrant. Cleopatra* was the most talked-about, written-about, and heavily advertised film of the year; to miss it was considered a social disaster.

When *Cleopatra* went out on the road, Theda agreed to do a personal appearance tour in several locales, including Florida, although she dreaded speaking before theater audiences. The tour was brightened up somewhat by Art Acord, the young cowboy who had played a minor role in *Cleopatra.* Acord — who later went on to become a film star himself — was demonstrating some rope tricks outside a theater when Theda's chauffeur called him a "Montgomery Ward cowboy." Acord promptly beat the tar out of the chauffeur. According to one eyewitness, Theda was properly impressed.

6 / The Girl of the Golden West

The same month that *Cleopatra* was released, an event occurred which brought home how important one star could be to a studio. Florence LaBadie had been the mainstay of New Rochelle's Thanhouser Studios since she joined them in 1911. The beautiful blonde actress starred in well over a hundred films, refusing to leave the studio even after the owner died in 1914 and Thanhouser's fortunes began to decline. Other stars decamped, but LaBadie's films continued to be as important to Thanhouser as Theda's were to Fox. Then, on October 13, 1917, Florence LaBadie died at age twenty-nine from injuries sustained in an auto accident. LaBadie's death took the heart out of the company. Thanhouser was out of business within a year. William Fox had other stars, but the lesson of LaBadie could not have been lost on him.

Cleopatra fever abating, Theda was soon back in the studio (still in Los Angeles, to her dismay), filming a rather clever spy drama called *The Rose of Blood*. It was her first Russian Revolution film, a genre that had become quite popular since the uprising. By the time *The Rose of Blood* was filmed in the autumn of 1917, Russia had dropped out of the war, Czar Nicholas had abdicated, the royal family was being held prisoner in Siberia, and all hell was generally breaking loose between the Red and White armies.

The Rose of Blood's author and co-star, Richard Ordynski, was a musical director of the Metropolitan Opera, and came up with a plot worthy of the most lurid opera. Lisza Tapenka (Theda) is a poor Russian girl who weds a Prime Minister. She is soon recruited by the Revolution and, according to one review, "wrecks hearts, railroad trains, slays one after another and concludes the fifth reel by blowing up the separate peace cabinet, which includes her husband." The rose of the title was the trademark which Lisza left on each of her victims.

Left: As Russian Revolutionary Lisza Tapenka in *The Rose of Blood* (1917). *Photo: Archive Photos. Right:* Portrait still from *The Rose of Blood. Photo: Joseph P. Eckhardt, Lisa Bulger.*

Though a much smaller and less pretentious film than *Cleopatra, The Rose of Blood* did quite well when it opened in November. The plot was silly but engaging, and Theda, according to *Photoplay*, "is so much more convincing than in her *Cleopatra* that you hardly know her for the same actress" (oddly, *Photoplay* had given Theda a rave in *Cleopatra* — they must have changed reviewers between films). Chicago didn't get to see *The Rose of Blood*; censors banned it entirely, claiming the film might incite susceptible Illinois citizens to overthrow the U. S. government.

By the time that film had opened, Theda was back in New York, reunited with her family to take a big step: she legally adopted her stage name. That in itself was not unusual, but in this case, the whole Goodman family followed along. Lori noted to reporters that she too hoped to become an actress, and Marque stated rather vaguely that he was in "the theatrical business." Still listing her address as 500 West End Avenue, Theda explained to Judge Donnelly that Bara was, after all, a diminution of the family name Baranger. The name change was promptly granted. As of November 18, 1917, the Goodmans officially became the Baras.

That same month, Theda was hijacked into viewing a multi-cultural vamp pageant at the Lyric Theater. She bowed and smiled graciously, but managed to get out of making a speech before the great Vampire Parade began. Among the contestants, according to *The New York American*, were Senorita Lupita Perea,* "famed throughout the Republic of Mexico for her deadly beauty and charm," Yosan, "who said she was a Chinese vampire," Blanche Johnson, "the most renowned Ethiopian enchantress of Harlem," and Mme. Yenika Lupotosky, who "claimed supremacy among Russian vampires."

It was a busy month. When not judging vamp contests, Theda was attending the theater. It was during this trip that she snatched one of Florenz Ziegfeld's costume designers from under his nose. Up until this point, Theda's costumes had either been purchased in shops by the actress herself or had been supplied by Fox's over-worked and understaffed wardrobe department. But on this trip to New York in late 1917, Theda discovered a twenty-one-year-old costume designer named George Hopkins. Hopkins, a Pasadena native, had begun his career designing magazine covers and had moved on to the *Ziegfeld Follies*. The young man was also a promising writer, and Theda snapped him up. Fox, for his part, was delighted to get a costumer designer and scenario writer for the price of one.

George Hopkins (nicknamed "Neje") designed all of Theda's costumes from *Madame DuBarry* till the end of her reign at Fox; he

---

Sic; the reporter probably meant "Perez."

Left: As Madame DuBarry (1918). *Right:* Outside Theda's dressing room during filming of *Madame DuBarry*. Photos: Robert S. Birchard.

also contributed to many of her screenplays. "I'm afraid I pay very little attention to historical detail," he admitted sheepishly to a reporter in 1919. "For instance, when I designed her costumes for *DuBarry*, I didn't worry about the exact kind of clothes they wore in those days. I just got the silhouette correctly and filled the rest in myself."

This somewhat lackadaisical attitude certainly didn't hurt George Hopkins' career. Theda's protegé went on to become a set designer and was nominated for an impressive thirteen Oscars, winning for his work on *A Streetcar Named Desire, My Fair Lady, Who's Afraid of Virginia Woolf?* and *Hello, Dolly!*.

In late 1917, while *Cleopatra* was still playing to packed houses around the country, Theda was back in California busy filming yet another historical "Super Production" (the title given to all of Theda's big-budget films). *Madame DuBarry* had been filmed two years earlier by stage star Mrs. Leslie Carter, but Fox threw caution

Two light-hearted moments from Madame DuBarry. *Left photo: Jerry Ohlinger. Right photo: Archive Photos.*

to the winds and assigned Theda her own version.

Theda, as usual, ran to the library and researched the life and death of poor DuBarry, one of the saddest victims of the French Revolution. Born Jeanne Bécu, the illegitimate daughter of a cook, the girl rose to become the mistress of Louis XV. Good-natured, blowzy, and big-hearted, DuBarry's star fell with the ascendence of Louis XVI and Marie Antoinette. She was arrested during the Terror and was dragged crying and screaming to the guillotine at the age of fifty.

Despite Theda's best efforts, George Hopkins' policy prevailed: *Madame DuBarry*'s historical accuracy was sacrificed for good theater. When the film was released in January, 1918, *Moving Picture World*'s reviewer noted, "it is a picture for Theda Bara followers rather than one for a college class or a literary club."

Happily, there were a lot of Theda Bara followers (among them, probably, a few college classes), and *DuBarry* was a hit. The

149

sight of Theda in her more-or-less historical costumes and blonde wigs provided the newspapers and fan magazines with great photo opportunities. "Doesn't she look Oskaloosa in this wig?" asked *The Chicago Tribune* in now-impenetrable slang.

But her performance was more than costumes and wigs: even Mae Tinee had to grudgingly pay Theda a very backhanded compliment. "Without having been imbued with any great amount of enthusiasm by Miss Bara's impersonation of Madame DuBarry," Tinee sniped, "I still maintain that it is the best thing the lady has ever done." *The Boston Post* had no such reservations, praising "the brilliant work of Theda Bara, who grasped the subtleties of the character in a most wonderful way."

DuBarry was a big enough hit for Fox to start planning another historical Super Production for Theda: writers and costumers began working on *Salome*, scheduled for filming in the summer of 1918. Meanwhile, a handful of programmers had to be gotten out of the way to pay the bills and keep Theda in front of the public every minute.

Theda had spent the winter holidays in New York with her family, but was rushed back to California in January 1918 to begin filming *The Forbidden Path*. While changing trains in Chicago, she told one reporter that the film was "much bigger than anything she has yet done," though she knew all too well that *The Forbidden Path* was just so much fluff about yet another Greenwich Village model. She played a sweet girl chosen to model as the Madonna and led to perdition by the artist who hired her. She becomes a debauched trollop, and years later is hired by the same artist to model as "the wreck of humanity."

Selig and Goldfrap planted a romantic story, an unusual tactic for them. Only one paper, *The Cleveland Leader*, bothered picking up on it. Reporter Joe Williams breathlessly told his readers of Theda's unnamed boyfriend. "We don't know who the astoundingly courageous chap is," Williams admitted, "except that he is an

As The Magdalene in *The Forbidden Path* (1918). *Photo: Michael Ankerich.*

easterner and that he is supposed to be almost entirely surrounded by United States government bonds." No further word was heard of this suitor, who was almost certainly invented to cover Theda's lack of a social life.

She may not have had a gentleman friend, but an event occurred while filming *The Forbidden Path* that proved to Theda that she had a lot of genuine admirers. One day on the set, Theda received a telegram that meant more to her than all her good reviews. Still pressed lovingly in her crumbling scrapbook, it reads:

> Feb. 11, 1918: 158th Infantry Regiment selected you for its Godmother by unanimous vote today. This Regiment composed of Arizona men all sincere admirers of yourself. Mary Pickford has adopted 143rd Artillery Regiment here. Will be greatly disappointed if you turn us down. Please wire your acceptance at once.

Theda had been keeping abreast of war news since 1914; she shopped at war bazaars, donated costumes and mementos to celebrity auctions. Her brother Marque, she proudly noted, was stationed at Fort Sill, Oklahoma, in the Signal Corps. In April 1917, Theda was asked to autograph the flag carried into battle by a company of volunteers from York, Pennsylvania. As a thank-you gift, the men (obviously unaware of her religion) sent her an ebony communion cup.

But the request from the 158th Infantry touched Theda beyond measure, and she adopted the boys as her own. When she finally had the chance to meet them en masse in June 1918, Theda broke down and wept as she addressed her boys in person. The Regiment presented arms to her as she sobbed happily, "my heart is too full — words can't come. This has been the most glorious day of my whole life." The boys of the 158th — bringing new meaning to the words "Army Camp" — responded by re-writing their marching song, doing their maneuvers to "Vamp, Vamp, Vamp, The Boys are Marching."

By early 1918, the U. S. had been committed to the European conflict for about nine months, and the film industry was all geared up to help the war effort. Peace-loving films like *Intolerance* and *Civilization* (both 1916) were now booed out of theaters, while new, more bloodthirsty fare like *To Hell with the Kaiser, Hearts of the World, The Beast of Berlin*, and *My Four Years in Germany* played to packed houses. One of the most bizarre war films was *Yankee Doodle in Berlin*, a Mack Sennett comedy featuring Bothwell Browne in female drag and Marie Prevost in male drag.

War efforts were much more insular than in World War Two: not many major stars joined the armed forces, though some tried; and it was difficult for American performers to entertain overseas troops (no international flights). Stars with German-sounding names swiftly changed them: Margarita Fischer became Margarita Fisher, Alfred Vosburgh became Alfred Whitman, and Norman Kaiser wisely became Norman Kerry. Even sauerkraut was renamed "Liberty Cabbage" for the duration. Perversely, Erich von Stroheim rose to fame by playing evil Germans, gaining the nickname The Man You Love to Hate.

Studios formed their own "home guards," both to train employees who might be sent overseas, and to guard the coastline in the unlikely event of a submarine attack. The actors and crew took these exercises very seriously. "Everyone was very patriotic," remembered Jesse Lasky, Jr. "Mrs. De Mille and Mary Pickford and everyone were all rolling bandages and wearing nurses costumes around Hollywood looking for wounded." When Honorary Colonel Pickford presented the Lasky Home Guard with their silk flag, she wore "a splendid couturier's outfit of patriotic grey with a little veil down the back," recalled Agnes DeMille. "She looked splendid . . . and sent them to death very valiantly. The grisly part is, some *did* go to death."

Theda, as a first-generation American, took great pride in her war work. She appeared at a "movie star day" at a northern California Army base in 1918, meeting General Pershing and former President Taft. Theda, Marie Dressler, Pickford, Fairbanks, and Chaplin were the most effective bond salespeople of the era, drawing huge crowds at every stop. In the fall of 1917, Theda hawked Liberty Loan Bonds in front of the New York Public Library on Fifth Avenue and 41st Street; she sold $70,000 in one afternoon and was congratulated in person by President Wilson. So successful a saleswoman was Theda that the Stage Women's War Relief asked her to return in November, when she sold another $300,000 worth of Bonds. Back in Los Angeles, she drew another huge crowd at a Bond Rally in April 1918.

The studio was not adverse to using the war for their own publicity efforts, of course. When German-occupied territory was recaptured by the Allies, Fox announced that bootleg copies of *A Fool There Was*, *Cleopatra* and *Under the Yoke* were discovered to have been screened and enjoyed by the evil Hun (no doubt other studios released the same story about their own films). In 1918, Theda met with Judge Louis Lazard of the Brussels Board of Commerce, who enthused, "she is a remarkable woman, and I have occasion to know that she is the idol of the Belgian populace, especially among those who are at the present time in England." He went on to imply that the main reason the war must be won was so Belgian people could see Theda Bara movies on their own soil.

A story was also released that Theda had dreamed of the war being brought to an end through a woman's influence. "If you or I ventured to state we had a vision in which we saw peace in the world war restored by a woman," snapped *The Cleveland Plain*

Dealer, "we would be looked upon with tolerant commiseration by our friends, and perhaps clapped into the nearest nutty shanty by our enemies."

Theda's next film, *The Soul of Buddha,* was notable only for the claim that Theda wrote the story. According to a press release, "Miss Bara wrote [*The Soul of Buddha*] on the train coming from California to New York and scenario experts at once pronounced it a big winner."

The press notes go on to state that Theda was inspired to write the story by reading of the execution of Dutch-born dancer Mata Hari, who died on October 15, 1917, and that "this conjured up in my mind the many mysteries of the Far East. Never having portrayed a character of that sort, I determined to make use of my time in planning a scenario embracing this feature."

There is no indication, of course, that Theda wrote or even suggested the story; certainly it bears the mark of Adrian Johnson, who wrote more than a dozen of Theda's scenarios. As Theda had never before — and never again — professed any interest in screenwriting, it's very unlikely that she had a hand in *The Soul of Buddha.* There *is* an outside possibility that Lori Bara wrote it, as she went on to become a successful screenwriter in the 1930's.

The results were pretty woeful. *The Soul of Buddha* told the story of Bavahari, an unwilling Buddhist priestess (alternately described in reviews as "Javanese" and "Japanese"), who elopes to England with an army man. She is pursued by a vengeful Buddhist priest, who is "unobserved, despite the fact that he wears a Turkish towel wrapped about his head and rolls the whites of his eyes right in broad daylight" (this from the ever-sarcastic Mae Tinee). Bavahari becomes a celebrated dancer — a la Mata Hari — and is murdered

Left: Theda sold $70,000 of Liberty Loan Bonds in front of the New York Public Library in November of 1917. *Photo: Jerry Ohlinger. Right: The Soul of Buddha* (1918) didn't amount to much, but Theda confiscated this statue. *Photo: Archive Photos.*

dramatically onstage by the determined and overacting priest.

Obviously, Fox was not worried about offending Buddhists. Selig and Goldfrap suggested that theater owners scatter "Hindu Death Signs" and statues of Buddha around to add to the general atmosphere. As a publicity stunt, Theda was persuaded to attend a Buddhist ceremony with Lori and afterwards declared to reporters that she'd converted to Buddhism (nothing was ever heard of this again, and the reaction of her Jewish relatives must be left to the imagination).

The Great Mysterious East was once again Fort Lee, New Jersey, where *The Soul of Buddha* was filmed in the cold December of 1917. One of the most important sets was the pile of papier-mâché rocks representing some kind of "Javanese Buddhist" altar. The rocks proved a little too realistic for a local goat, who would try to climb them every night, fall through and get caught, only to be found bleating piteously the next morning. The goat, nick-named Betsy, was adopted by the Fox company and happily trailed Theda from her dressing room to the set. Another unexpected hang-up came with a baby actor who took two hours to fall asleep and play dead — no one was dispatched to simply buy a baby doll; Edwards sat stone-faced, trying to will the baby to sleep as the cast tip-toed around delicately.

The film didn't cost much money and more than made back its investment. Reviewers one and all hated it. Mae Tinee, of course, got her licks in, calling *The Soul of Buddha* "a sodden conglomera-tion entirely uninteresting and unoriginal, with Miss Bara finally dying an air-clawing death." "It is difficult to take either Miss Bara or the picture seriously," agreed Louella Parsons. One Wisconsin paper admitted the film was, perhaps, "interesting," while a Cleve-land reviewer threw up his hands, stating that Theda "simply vamps all over the place."

The only good that came out of the film was a lovely Buddha statue, which Theda appropriated for her own apartment.

Under the Yoke, filmed in California in the spring of 1918, was billed as "a romantic melodrama of the Philippine revolution" of 1900. Theda played a wealthy Spanish girl living in the Philippines when the revolution broke out; her character winds up saving her lover from a wicked plantation owner.

Vamp: The Rise and Fall of Theda Bara

It was an exciting shoot, for all the wrong reasons: ten extras were injured filming the revolution scenes and an earthquake hit California during production (Theda, happily, only lost some china). The film itself, however, was no better than *The Soul of Buddha* and played out its three-day runs without causing a stir.

Theda and Albert Roscoe as star-crossed lovers in *Under the Yoke* (1918). *Photos: Robert S. Birchard.*

The height of fashion, ca. 1918. *Photo: Gene Andrewski.*

Chapter 7

The Edge of the Abyss

By this time, Theda had worked her way well into popular culture. In the late 1910's, scores of vamp songs paying tribute to Theda were written. It's notable that almost all of these were comedy songs. Vaudeville comics and review producers spoofed Theda's image, to the delight of record-buyers and audiences. One dancing school even invented The Vampire Walk, though the step never really caught on, even in that tango- and two-step-crazed era. Theda's own vampire walk, Fox assured the press, was taught to her by her "warm friend" Isadora Duncan.

One hit song of 1919, *The Vamp*, urged listeners, "Everybody do the vamp — vamp until you get a cramp!" The unhappy family in *Rebecca's Back from Mecca* lamented, "She's as bold as Theda Bara; Theda's bare but Becky's barer . . ." The singer of *I'm a Jazz Vampire* bragged, "Went down to the river, stood on the bank; shook my shoulders and the boats all sank." In the Broadway show *Leave It to Jane*, "Cleo-patterer" was described thus: "On every man that wandered by, she gave the Theda Bara eye . . ." Neighbors complained of *Sally Greene, the Village Vamp*, "you should see her raise the dickens; she's vamping all the cows and chickens!" As late as 1923, Sophie Tucker was singing, "My kissing men can't resist; when I kiss 'em they stay kissed. They call me Vampin' Sal, the Sheik of Georgia!"

One typical song was *Since Sarah Saw Theda Bara* (to be sung with a Yiddish accent):

Every night Sarah Cohn would go
To a moving picture show
And there she saw upon the screen
Miss Theda Bara, the "Vampire Queen."
She saw men fall for her dev'lish smile,
But she fooled them all the while.
Then Sarah said, "it's an easy game,
I think I can do just the same!"

Since Sarah saw Theda Bara, she became a holy terror.
Oi, how she tears her hair, Oi, then sings, "I don't care!"
She will break a heart each night,
Just to raise an appetite.
She'll take you and try to break you,
Then like a Vampire she'll "vamp" away;
One kiss from her and you are done,
'Cause her lips, they are just like chloroform!
Since Sarah saw Theda Bara,
She's a wera, wera dangerous girl.

Theda's image decorates sheet music, mid-1910's. *Left photos: Museum of Modern Art. Above photo: Mary Anne Styburksi.*

Comedienne Fanny Brice had already parodied Theda in the 1916 *Ziegfeld Follies.* John De Koven in *The Cleveland Leader* wrote that "when Miss Brice has done, Theda is thrown, eyes and all, to the lions to make a Ziegfeld holiday. It is a symphony of so many snakey maneuvers, so staggering an assortment of amorous wiggles, so luscious a collection of lip-twisting and eye-rolling — in fine, so gorgeous and grim a grotesquery that it is almost libel, and the original Theda might be ill over it. . . . Her impersonation as it stands in these first days of the new *Follies* is veritably an irresistible rib-tickler, but by the same token it is unmitigatingly cruel." Theda's response — if she saw the show — was not recorded for posterity. The fact that Brice also lampooned Isadora Duncan may have been some small comfort.

For all the kidding, the myth of the vampire woman was still alive and well in 1918. That year, Theda was subpoenaed to give testimony in what had to be the most outrageous "blame the victim" murder trial of its time. One George Martinez of San Francisco had tossed his wife, Rosa Aguilar, out of a window. His lawyer attempted to call Theda to the stand as an expert witness, stating that the victim was actually a vampire "who ruled imperiously the social functions of the Plaza and parts of Chinatown." Aguilar had, claimed the defense, lost her heart to Martinez and thrown herself out the window, her vamping days at an end. Not surprisingly, the judge decided against calling Theda to the stand.

Theda spent most of the early summer of 1918 in the deserts of California filming *Salome*, her biggest-budget film since *Cleopatra* a year earlier.

The film industry was swiftly changing, and the competition was a lot stiffer. Her biggest rivals in 1918 were still Charlie Chaplin and Mary Pickford. Pickford, releasing through Famous Players, had recently had a huge hit with *Poor Little Rich Girl* and was about to release *Stella Maris*. Chaplin's successful *Shoulder Arms* was about to be released by First National. Lillian and Dorothy Gish, working happily under D. W. Griffith, were making *Hearts of the World* in Europe. Alla Nazimova was making highbrow films for Metro, while at Select, Norma Talmadge and Clara Kimball Young got the respectable dramatic roles Theda craved.

Nineteen eighteen was a banner year for films: *Tarzan of the Apes* was one of the big hits, along with Mabel Normand's *Mickey* and the comedies of "Fatty" Arbuckle and Buster Keaton. A lot of newcomers were pushing their way into the industry as well, people who would carry their fame into the 1920's and beyond. By 1918, Rudolph Valentino, Colleen Moore, Bebe Daniels, Tallulah Bankhead, Chester Morris, and Billie Burke were already appearing in films.

Nineteen eighteen was also a banner year for Theda: on May

25, her annual raise went into effect, giving her a salary of $4,000 a week (plus a percentage of her film rentals). As well as being paid like a star, Theda began to act like one.

Except for *Salome*, the budgets of her films had dropped, along with the quality of the stories: *The Soul of Buddha* and *Under the Yoke* were cheap, silly films not worthy of Fox's greatest star, and Theda's temper was wearing a bit thin. Riding high on *Salome*, she began to throw her weight around.

Theda had discovered that no work really started on her films till mid-afternoon; she showed up on the set early in the morning and sat around for hours waiting for lights to be set, extras to be corralled. By the time she started shooting *Salome*, she laid down the law in a way which not even Garbo attempted: Theda Bara would show up on the set at 1:00 P.M. sharp, and everything had better be ready for her. J. Gordon Edwards agreed to her demands, and shot her co-stars and crowd scenes in the morning. At 1:00, Theda would pull up in her limousine, accompanied by a maid and perhaps her sister. She would pleasantly breeze onto the set and give her all until sundown, then steal away home.

There was surprisingly little ill will on the set about this. "You do more work in one hour than most o' them birds does in a week," one electrician told Theda; a newspaper reporter watching her film agreed that "she does more work in the afternoon than the average star will do in a week, because she is ready to go on, and she knows exactly what she is supposed to do."

Salome, like Cleopatra, was a woman whose story begged to be filmed. The daughter of Herodius, who demanded John the Baptist's head on a platter, she had been the subject of plays (notably Oscar Wilde's) and films long before Theda got hold of her. Since the story was Biblical, Fox hoped to get around the censors. Fox's version was based on the chronicles of Josephus, with a little nudge from Wilde and screenwriter Adrian Johnson. George Hopkins came up with the most bizarre costumes since *Cleopatra*:

Vamp: The Rise and Fall of Theda Bara

Salome (1918). *Photos: Robert S. Birchard.*

nearly invisible chiffon scarves, one dress made of discreetly draped pearls; and another bedecked with so many silk grapes that Theda looked like a vamp salad. In those days before sunscreen, the pale-skinned actress had to take cover under tents between shots to avoid a serious burn.

Theda was at her slimmest in this film, having lost at least twenty pounds. Still stung by the remarks over her figure when *Cleopatra* was released, she recalled, "I thought I was a little too fat for the costumes . . . so I took a course in Dr. Somebody-or-other's Reducing Exercises. I gained twelve pounds!" Strenuous dieting got her down to about 115 pounds by the time *Salome* started shooting.

She also wore a very heavy and uncomfortable black shoulder-length wig for this film, though why her own waist-length hair wouldn't do is something of a mystery. Theda had originally wanted to be a blonde Salome, she told *Motion Picture Classics* reporter Martha Groves McKelvie. "I wanted to be a different

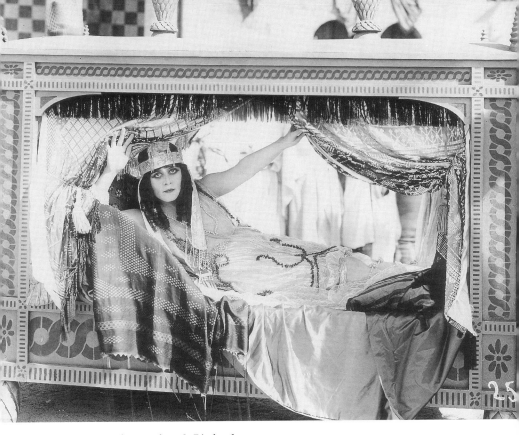

As Salome. *Photo: Robert S. Birchard.*

Salome," she sighed, "so I ordered the wig-maker to send me a wig of tawny, blonde hair. It was to be almost like a lion's mane, wild, unruly and weird. But the man had no imagination. He sent me one with Pickford curls. So I'm a brunette Salome, after all."

One on-the-set reporter has left us with a fascinating glimpse at how big-budget crowd scenes were filmed in 1918. After Salome dances her famous dance, the king's banquet hall is destroyed by a divinely inspired storm; the scene involved three hundred extras, twelve mounted airplane propellers to supply the wind, and all the assistant directors Edwards could summon up. While the propellers were being tested, several of the extra girls, noted the reporter,

> looked exactly as if they wished they had not tried to get into the pictures by the extra route.

Salome. Photo above: Jerry Ohlinger. Photo below: Robert S. Birchard.

Assistant directors passed from group to group, giving instructions. Grape juice was passed around. Some bees from a neighboring orange grove came over to see what was going on, and a little flurry of excitement ensued . . . More extras came in — handsome youths wearing Roman tunics. They were stationed down in front near the cameras, where there were several girls without partners. "Make friends with these girls," said the director, "and when the feast gets going, make love to them."

One bashful Roman took a place on the divan near a buxom looking extra of the opposite sex. "How do you do?" she said, putting out her hand. "My name's Robinson," he said. "Glad to meet you. I guess I'll have to make love to you — if you don't mind." "I should worry," the girl replied.

Finally, Theda herself arrived on the set, much to the excitement of all present.

A hush fell over the scene. "Look!" said a hundred voices. "There she is!" All eyes turned to the throne. . . . "Oh, isn't she lovely?" cried several girlish voices. Miss Bara was inspecting the scene. Much attention was paid to her. King Herod got down from his throne, and even the great Edwards came down from the directing stand and consulted with her.

Rehearsal started. The crowd drank their grape juice. They got to their feet and shouted a health to the king. But it was too tame. Assistants passed here and there, talking, exhorting and urging them to greater efforts. They tried it again with no greater success. And then Edwards, heretofore silent except when he gave orders to his assistants, got into the game. He stood on the edge of his high platform.

"Get life into this," he shouted. "Remember where you are. You are back in Jerusalem, over 2000 years ago. You are at the palace of the king. You are having a feast. You are glad — you are merry — you are carefree. Now! Drink, drink! laugh!

Portrait still from *Salome*. *Photo: Robert S. Birchard.*

talk! Drink to the health of the king! Drain your glasses. Drink again!" The scene livened up. Edwards was making them believe it. Music from an orchestra hidden somewhere on the side lines was heard. Edwards talked and exhorted again, and — miraculously — the whole thing became real ! . . . The bashful Roman youth whose name was Robinson threw his arms around the buxom extra girl and kissed her. The scene was alive. The crowd was hypnotized by the thing.

Theda then went into her dance, flinging white chiffon veils to the winds and bending to kiss a very unconvincing papier-mâché head on a golden charger. At this point, propmen turned on the propellers and began flashing fake lightning at the set.

The directors, no longer able to be heard, scuttled away out of the awful blasts of wind. The people in the set did not need to be told what to do now. They knew they were supposed to be scared and must get away from the banquet hall as soon as possible, and they stood not upon the order of their going, but fell over one another and everything else in their way — and went.

The crowd was absolutely wild. A thousand veils and articles of clothing filled the air. Couches and divans were overturned. Head dresses, turbans, went flying here and there. Romans lost their tunics, wise men lost their robes, vestal virgins lost their vestments. The bashful Roman, Robinson, tried to save his stout partner, and she tried to save him, but he broke away, turned a handspring over a divan and was gone.

By mid-1918, Theda was no longer the only ace in William Fox's deck. That year, he hired cowboy star Tom Mix. The handsome, personable Mix had been a popular western and adventure star since 1911; his addition to the Fox stock players was a real coup. By the end of the silent era, he'd made a fortune for himself and Fox with countless hits like *Western Blood* (1918), *The Wilderness Trail* (1919), *Just Tony* (1922), *Dick Turpin* and *Riders of the Purple Sage* (both 1925), and *The Last Trail* (1927). Even better for Fox — but not for Theda — Tom Mix westerns cost nearly nothing to produce and brought in huge profits. They were derided by critics, but the young male audience couldn't get enough of them.

Fox began branching out, producing more sure-fire westerns with William Farnum and George Walsh. By the late 1910's, the Fox stock players also included popular performers Dustin Farnum, Colleen Moore, June Caprice, and Theda's arch-rival Miriam Cooper. Fox also signed Evelyn Nesbit, the scandalous dancer whose husband, Harry K. Thaw, had murdered her lover, architect Stanford White. This real-life vamp's career failed after her notoriety had died down and she soon vanished from sight.

Theda wasn't worried yet; she was still one of the biggest stars in the country that season. In August 1918, *Motion Picture* held a popularity contest; the results drive home the fleetness and instability of fame. "The Greatest and Most Permanent of All Contests," as the magazine modestly titled it, surprised even the editors. Theda came in tenth, with 42,714 votes, after such stars as Mary Pickford (#1), Douglas Fairbanks (#3) and William S. Hart (#5). But Theda also finished lower than Marguerite Clark (#2), Harold Lockwood (#4) and Anita Stewart (#8), players now considered to be fairly minor and unimportant.

More surprising are the dismal scores received by performers now considered superstars of the period: Charlie Chaplin (#17), Lillian Gish (#69), Mabel Normand (#115). And even the most diligent of film historians will be amazed to see some of the long-forgotten players who earned thousands of votes from star-struck fans: Carol Holloway, Edward Langford, Mahlon Hamilton, Violet Mersereau — once celebrated in "The Greatest and Most Permanent of All Contests," now anonymous names in a faded fan magazine.

Salome was unusual in that it was released in August; most of Theda's huge blockbusters (*Carmen*, *Romeo and Juliet*, *Cleopatra*) were released in the fall. Air conditioning did not arrive in theaters until the 1920's, so summer months were very slow for both films and the legitimate stage. Many theaters had a summer policy of mixing films and vaudeville (Theda's *The Eternal Sapho* was accompanied in Philadelphia by an act tantalizingly called "Adonis and His Dog: A Study in Lavender"). "The new season" began in the autumn, when the temperature cooled down and audiences were starved for entertainment after their summer hiatus — the premiering of new TV shows in the fall is a holdover from this tradition. The scheduling of *Salome* in August certainly held down receipts.

Still, the film did very well and gained Theda even better notices than *Cleopatra*. Fox had George Rubenstein write a score for the film, which was shipped off to theaters along with the reels. While one Roman history scholar complained that the architecture was too Egyptian (leftovers from *Cleopatra*?) and that the princess Salome didn't have enough attendants, most critics were well pleased with the extravagant film and with the star. "Theda Bara is in her element as the arch vampire who finds little or no difficulty in luring every man to destruction that strikes her fancy," said one paper.

Another paper took Theda to task for not being "intellectual" enough in her portrayal. Theda, who read every review avidly, good and bad, pitched a fit. "Will I have subtitles to show my brainy sayings?" she asked Frederick James Smith of *Motion Picture Classics*. "Or will I go thru the dance of the seven veils with a finger thoughtfully pressed to my forehead?!"

Theda took ill after filming *Salome* and stayed home for a month, nursed by her mother and Lori (her extreme weight loss for *Salome* may have weakened her system). Fox released a notice to the press that Theda was out "mountain climbing," but the star, non-athletic even when in the best of health, lay at home reading scripts sent to her by the studio. None of them seemed worth getting out of bed for.

Right after *Salome* Theda was dumped into *When a Woman Sins*, yet another haphazard vamp programmer. Advertised rather baldly in trade hand-outs as "The Play That Means a Fat Bank Bal-

Albert Roscoe tending to Theda in *When a Woman Sins* (1918). *Photo: Archive Photos.*

ance," the film cast Theda as nursemaid to an elderly roué; she falls in love with her charge's son, a divinity student (Albert Roscoe). Complications arise, of course; the old man dies, a cousin kills himself over her, and Theda becomes a notorious dancer named Poppea. Just as she's about to kill herself at a wild party, the young divine comes through and proclaims his love for her.

Anxious to sell this one on the heels of *Salome*'s success, Fox advertised *When a Woman Sins* with catchlines like, "a thrilling drama of a wronged girl's struggle against the hypocrisy of society" and "her siren's soul longed for love," and suggested all kinds of wild stunts for theater owners, including dressing girl ushers up as nursemaids. They also told theater managers to place lilies and poppies in the lobby with a sign reading, "the poppies of pleasure, or the pure lilies of chastity: which is your choice?" They suggested "you persuade the pastor of a church in your city to preach a sermon on the lesson of the picture" (an interesting thought, as the vamp emerges triumphant in the final reel). Not surprisingly, one obliging — and unnamed — priest proclaimed via Fox, "I wish every girl in America could see this film."

Money was certainly poured into *When a Woman Sins*. Theda wore what was passed off as "a five-thousand-dollar gown from a Fifth Avenue modiste" (no doubt George Hopkins), and one church interior employed the services of five hundred extras. Most critics hated it; as usual, Mae Tinee hated it more than most. "It's about as punk as most of the photoplays in which I have been so unfortunate as to witness Miss Bara," she said. "In a Bara picture . . . it must all be Bara. You can see that everybody in the cast understands that and they slink furtively on the edges of the lime-light voicing their meaows and woof-woofs apologetically." The most loyal of Theda's fans still lined up at the box office, but receipts were beginning to fall off.

Theda's films languished during the late fall and early winter of 1918/1919, but the reason was not the end of World War One. Along with the good news of Armistice came the Spanish influenza. Film and stage shows closed, people wore cotton masks out on the streets, and the disgusting habit of spitting became a punishable offense. In October, 1918, one hundred ninety-six thousand people died of the flu in America alone. By the time the epidemic had subsided in 1919, as many as forty million people world wide had succumbed. The film community lost, among others, leading man Harold Lockwood, rising actress Tessie Harron (younger sister of Robert), and director John Collins.

Lillian Gish later recalled her own bout with the flu, while in pre-production for *Broken Blossoms*. "I thought I'd better walk home, as maybe the exercise would make me feel better," Gish later recounted. "I was so weak I had to crawl under a bush to get the strength to go a little further. [The next day], I had a temperature of 106 and was delirious. . . . I went back to rehearsals before I had recovered completely." Griffith had Gish rehearse in a surgical mask, which must have tried even his directorial abilities.

So it was no small act of bravery for Theda to visit veteran's hospitals that fall and winter, with the flu raging. She refused to wear a gauze face mask, insisting that the patients deserved better than that.

Theda was actually excited about her next film, *The She-Devil*, as Fox promised to incorporate some comedy into the script. Press releases made much of the vamp's first venture into comedy, though it really only involved a scene or two. Looking like "little Tottie Dewdrop" in a white chiffon gown and beaming with happiness, she gushed to a reporter, "have they told you the good news out at the studio? You know, I suppose, that I'm not a vampire? I'm making a Spanish comedy at the present time and the brilliant gayety of it all fairly thrills me."

Theda portrayed Lolette, a Spanish adventuress who falls in love with a French artist (Albert Roscoe). She and her lover endure several hair-raising adventures, outwitting a love-struck bandit (6'2", 210-pound opera singer George McDaniel). "Treat 'em rough! They like it!" proclaimed an unfortunate press placard, showing a photo of Theda being beaten soundly by McDaniel.

A twenty-thousand-dollar Spanish town — including a "working" river — was built in Hollywood for the film. Though an on-set fire cost two days' filming, the main aggravation in making *The She-Devil* came from the huge menagerie which populated the town: hundreds of sheep, goats, geese, pigs, oxen, donkeys and one bear. The bear had quite a pedigree, having formerly been the mascot of an infantry regiment at Camp Lewis, Washington. When they shipped off, the boys sent the animal — named "Theda Beara"

As the fiery Spanish Lolette in *The She-Devil* (1918). *Photo: The Everett Collection.*

— off to its namesake, where it promptly won a co-starring role not only in *The She-Devil*, but in several Tom Mix films. One of Theda's comedy scenes entailed feeding the bear with a baby bottle full of milk. After Edwards yelled, "cut!" Theda tried to yank the bottle away. Theda Beara, not quite finished, took a healthy swipe at Theda Bara. It was finally decided to ship the animal off to a local zoo.

A full complement of far-fetched stories were handed out to local newspaper offices to promote the film; in this case, it was said that Theda discovered the body of a murder victim while strolling casually around the set of *The She-Devil*. Amazingly, several newspapers printed this without investigating further.

The She-Devil might have been an interesting and successful film, with a light, outdoorsy character not unlike the one Theda had scored with in *Under Two Flags*. It may even have opened a new career path for her, had the comedy scenes been particularly effective. But *The She-Devil* was a victim of bad timing. It was released on November 10, 1918; the following day, the Armistice was signed. Few people went to any movies that week, and newspapers were too full of war news to bother with reviewing films — even films containing comedy sequences involving vamps and bears.

By this time, the picture-going public had a good sense of who Theda Bara was: a quiet, refined bookworm with a dry sense of humor. Even small-town newspapers, which generally printed Fox hand-outs verbatim, no longer bought the "born in the shadow of the Pyramids" nonsense, though they still regularly printed publicity stories and fake interviews without a tremor of remorse.

But it was the fan magazines and their intrepid reporters who gave a fairly accurate view of Theda and her fellow stars. Trade magazines, aimed at theater owners and film professionals, had existed since *Moving Picture World* had begun publishing in 1907. The first American magazine aimed at the movie fan, however, was *Motion Picture Story*, founded in 1911. It was soon followed by a flood of competitors, most of them pretty well written and supplied with excellent photography: *Photoplay, Motion Picture Classic* (one of the best; it was published from 1915 through 1931), *Picture Play, Shadowland* and others.

The magazines began by printing film plot synopses and portraits, but by the mid-teens they included interviews, industry news (who married whom, who signed up with what studio), question and answer columns (the most famous being *Motion Picture Classic*'s sarcastic and long-lived Answer Man), fashion spreads and write-in contests. Clever interviewers were able to get Theda to drop her studio line, become human and chat freely about books, her career, family, and everyday life. Her talks with fan magazine writers Wallace Franklin, Roberta Courtlandt, Delight Evans, Martha Groves McKelvie and Agnes Smith are both charming and revealing.

Nineteen-nineteen began with *The Light*, in which Theda played "the wickedest woman in Paris," quite an accomplishment when one considers the competition. Blanche DuMond ("she had eyes yet she saw not"), Theda's naughty Parisienne, becomes an Apache dancer after being rejected for service as a war nurse. She redeems herself in the end by nursing a blinded soldier from her past who, of course, doesn't know who she is.

The press agents at Fox must have been getting punchy by this time, issuing suggested taglines like, "the nimble feet of a dancer sent him skipping to perdition." They even had the incredibly poor taste to promote the film by re-publishing an essay by Helen Keller on blindness.

The Light was filmed back East, to Theda's relief, so she could open up her New York flat and catch up on the latest shows: Nazimova was doing Ibsen on Broadway, and young Tallulah Bankhead made her stage debut in *The Squab Farm*. Theda visited her favorite museums and did some shopping — mostly for books to take back with her to California.

The Light was not an easy shoot. Several scenes were filmed in the all-glass studio at Fort Lee, not far from a munitions factory in

Charles Hopkins contrived what appears to be a toothache hat for Theda in
The Light (1919). *Photo: The Everett Collection.*

Morgan, New Jersey. Rumors circulated constantly that the plant was about to explode — it never did, but the cast and crew were understandably jumpy, rushing outside in a panic every time an alarm sounded.

Shooting moved to New Orleans for a week or so, where Theda enjoyed the cornbread and French cooking, but hated the sultry heat. She was required to drive a race car at breakneck speed — no stuntman was requested, though Theda's driving skills were minimal at best. Racing through the streets, blind as a bat without her glasses, she somehow managed to avoid killing anyone or running off the road. "It was thoroughly exhilarating," she told a reporter on the set, "but I won't do a thing like this again!" Far from the munitions plant, an explosion did occur while filming a battle scene — one actor (non-union, of course) was wounded in the arm and shipped off to a local hospital.

The Light was a happy surprise after her last few duds. Business began to surge again, and reviews were generally favorable. The biggest surprise came when Theda got her one and only unrestrained rave from Mae Tinee, who said, "she really gets down to business . . . acts like a real human being, for which I for one am so sincerely grateful that I could almost embrace her."

Mae Tinee wasn't alone in praising Theda. That same month, a Japanese fan magazine, *Yeiga Sekai*, voted her the most popular star in that country (609,231 people cast ballots for Theda). Brazil's *Weekly Review* also noted that "Thedabaraism" had swept that country, that "society has bowed to the cult of this most fascinating woman."

Indeed, Theda was predicted to become the first movie star on Mars. Inventor Nikola Tesla was experimenting with sending photos by wireless to other planets, and promised that the first to be broadcast would be Theda Bara's. *Photoplay* agreed with the choice: "In addition to being seen daily by two hundred fifty thousand persons in moving picture theaters in this country, her portrait adorns some one million posters, and it is estimated that more than twenty million people have seen her photographs displayed in the newspapers of the United States." *Photoplay*, suspecting that Mars was inhabited, forecasted a whole new public for Theda.

So when she got a load of her next script, a melodrama called *When Men Desire*, Theda stormed into Fox's office. *When Men Desire* was a low-budget production, to be filmed on location in Princeton, New Jersey. Besides the cut-rate settings, Theda objected to the story, in which she played an American girl caught behind the lines in Germany when war broke out. World War One had ended a few months before and people were sick of the subject; war films were a dead issue and doing poorly at the box office. To hand Theda this scenario — which had obviously been sitting on the shelf at least a year — was not only a slap in the face, but it endangered her popularity.

She filmed *When Men Desire*, with no good will. The shoot itself was rather unpleasant: one of Theda's evil German attackers wrestled with her while wearing a big spiky Iron Cross. Theda, who wore only a rather thin gown and was known for putting a lot of enthusiasm into her fight scenes, received nine long gashes down her arms. "I hate to be scratched!" she grumbled. "But of all things I hate to be scratched by an Iron Cross, even if it is only a fake one."

The film predictably failed to draw customers. One of the few papers to bother reviewing it called *When Men Desire* "a crude and improbable melodrama . . . On the whole the picture is not up to even the mild standard of previous Bara offerings."

It finally happened, after four years: Theda's vogue was passing. The vamp film had been declared dead at least once a year since 1915, but this time there were some facts to back up the obituary. Theda's films were beginning to fail; as Tom Mix brought more money in to Fox, Theda was falling behind. The fact that she was being handed second-rate scripts and her budgets were being slashed accounted for the drop in box office receipts; but there was

As Marie Lohr, caught behind enemy lines, in *When Men Desire (1919)*. *Photo: Archive Photos.*

also the little matter of Theda's attitude. She just didn't care anymore. Although she and Edwards still got along well, Theda hated the stories she was being given and found it hard to disagree with reviewers who called her films tripe. She came to the set at one o'clock, went through the paces with increasing bad humor, and went home. It began to show on-screen.

She dreaded going to work. Theda commented bitterly, "the inefficiency is appalling. . . . Nothing was ever ready. We would wait for hours and hours until some carpenter had corrected a mistake in the setting. And all about you there is a grinding and a pounding. The mechanical staff have a way of blaming all the

Vamp: The Rise and Fall of Theda Bara

She was only a lighthouse keeper's daughter: with Alfred Fremont in *The Siren's Song* (1919). *Photo: Jerry Ohlinger.*

delays on the star. The star has no come-back because she cannot go and tell tales on men who need their day's wages. Mr. Fox seldom came to the studio; he was busy at the home office. I only saw him a few times a year."

To appease her, Fox put a little more money and thought into *The Siren's Song*, recreating a Breton village on Catalina Island in Southern California. The studio constructed a sixty-foot light-house, which the town bought and used after the film makers

Theda and William B. Davidson find love in the South Seas in *A Woman There Was* (1919). *Photo: The Everett Collection.*

packed up and went home. Theda tried to be a good sport, and joined the crew on fishing trips between shots, finding the whole thing very dull until she reeled in a twenty-pound yellowtail. The only real excitement came when she was knocked out of a boat by a large wave during filming. The crew hollered and prepared to dive in after her and the attending reporters began scribbling near-drowning stories, but Theda simply stood up in the knee-deep water and waded back to shore.

185

Vamp: The Rise and Fall of Theda Bara

All the money and new-found good will didn't help; *The Siren's Song* was another failure, as was her next film, *A Woman There Was*. Theda was assigned one last leading man, new to the Fox stock company: the rather bulky William B. Davidson joined Theda for *A Woman There Was* and co-starred in her two final Fox projects, hardly a happy time at the studio. Davidson, thirty-one, was the son of a New York judge and a graduate of NYU Law School, who'd run off to join the photoplays. He had co-starred with Pauline Frederick and John Barrymore before joining Fox. Davidson never became a star, but his career plodded along steadily through his last film, *The Farmer's Daughter*, in 1947.

Theda played Princess Zara of the South Seas in *A Woman There Was*, an unhappy choice of roles. She had gained back all the weight she had lost for *Salome* and more, and looked downright plump and homely in her grass skirts, short curly wig and dark makeup. Princess Zara was described in the script as "Amazonian" to get around Theda's heft, but that couldn't help the dim and dated story. Zara falls for a missionary, then takes a javelin in the midsection so he can go back to his nice white girlfriend in New England.

A Woman There Was, to no one's surprise, bombed when it opened in June 1919. Theda realized that her career just might be over.

Chapter 8

Gold Is Not All

Theda managed to get through late 1918 and early 1919 by searching for one last good film. After completing *A Woman There Was* she went home and stayed there while she, her family, and friends searched for a good, non-vamp script. "I went out on strike and I stayed `struck' until I had my way," she said. "I refused to vamp another single, solitary second unless I was first given the opportunity to prove I could be good just as easily as I was bad."

She appealed for sympathy through the press. "Five practically uninterrupted years of vamping had stretched my nerves pretty taut," she sighed to syndicated writer Jane Dixon. "I seldom had longer than a week between pictures, and even this was not my own. It was replete with dressmakers and costumers and period experts, a few days of intensive preparation for work to come." Theda carefully omitted the fact that her star schedule had her in front of the cameras only a few hours a day, and that she frequently vacationed in New York between films.

She did have one valid point, however; one vamp role after another was wearing her out. "Gradually those vampire emotions began to weigh me down," said Theda. "There were not enough laughs in my life, and I do so love to laugh."

All those vamps were wearing out Theda's welcome with audiences, too. Since *Salome* had been released in mid-1918, Theda had been handed one cheap, dreadful film after another. Receipts were falling, exhibitors were getting nervous about booking Bara films; even the much-lauded expensive look of her Theda Bara Super-Productions was falling off.

Vamp: The Rise and Fall of Theda Bara

No longer feeling harnessed by Fox's publicity men, Theda vented her anger to reporters: "Directors spend a great deal of money on unimportant things and then they economize in small ways that prove expensive in the end." Of the typecasting she was trying to leave behind, Theda said that "of course, there *is* no such thing as a vampire. No women are like that. That is why you can't get good stories for vampire pictures. They aren't real."

Theda suspected that her days at Fox were numbered, and that speaking her mind to the press would hasten her departure. She was also smart enough to know that no studio would venture signing her up unless she had a sure-fire hit to show them. A non-vamp hit.

The story she finally settled on, an Irish tale called *Kathleen Mavourneen*, had been popular for more than seventy years. Kathleen was a poor but plucky Irish girl celebrated in song (by Annie Crawford), poetry (by Tom Moore) and theater (a popular play by Dion Boucicault). *Kathleen Mavourneen* had been successfully filmed by Edison in 1906, but that release was long-forgotten by this time. The story — Theda's version, at any rate — would have been a good enough vehicle for any actress, from Mary Pickford to the Talmadge or Gish sisters. But it's difficult to tell why Theda pinned so many hopes on the film; the plot was really nothing special.

Theda played Kathleen, an Irish girl in the early nineteenth century, who is engaged to her poor but honest neighbor, Terrence O'Moore ("Mavourneen" was not her last name, but an Irish endearment). Kathleen is loved, pursued, and eventually kidnapped by the evil Squire of Tralee, who weds her by force. For some unfathomable reason, one of those annoying "it was all a dream" endings was tacked onto the film, with Kathleen back in the arms of Terrence.

Theda waxed lyrical about *Kathleen*. "This is the best role I've ever had," she enthused. "There isn't the slightest trace of the vam-

Kathleen Mavourneen tiptoes through the daisies (1919). *Photo: New York Public Library for the Performing Arts.*

pire in Kathleen, so you see I have kept my promise about the type of heroine I'd portray when I was ready to forsake the ladies of highly emotional proclivities. How I did delight in that quaint little Irish girl," she burbled. "I adopted her heart and soul. She permitted me to take down my hair . . . I no longer had to glide into a room and begin working the wiles of a trade as old as the call of sex. I could run and jump and skip and be happy."

Burning all bridges behind her, Theda went on to say that "the vampire woman of the screen is absurdly exaggerated. Sometimes she comes very close to being ridiculous instead of dangerous ... I will not slink and writhe and wriggle my eyes day in and day out. I demand to bob my curls and climb trees and love for love's own sake. I want to be, well, *natural*."

Theda was also to have a new director for her ambitious pet project. After twenty-three films together in four years, Theda and J. Gordon Edwards came to a parting of the ways. Edwards stayed with Fox, directing such films as *The Queen of Sheba, Nero,* and *The Shepherd King,* but he never really recaptured the success he'd had with Theda. He was semi-retired when he died of pneumonia on New Year's Eve, 1925, in New York's Plaza Hotel.

The man chosen to direct — and write — *Kathleen Mavourneen* was a tall, hawklike thirty-seven-year-old Englishman named Charles Brabin. Brabin was often referred to in the press as "Sir" or even "Lord" Brabin; he cultivated an upper-class accent and an upper-class charm which completely intimidated the culture-conscious film community. Theda, snob that she was, was impressed from the start.

"One morning they introduced us at the studio and informed me that he was going to direct my next picture," Theda recalled. "I thought he looked, well, sort of intelligent, don't you know? Not all directors — well, not all of them are what you'd call intelligent."

Brabin may well have been intelligent, but his background was as different from his public persona as Theda Bara's was from Theodosia Goodman. Both were poseurs, and this helped bring the two together in sympathy. Charles J. Brabin, Jr., was born in Liverpool on April 17, 1882. His father ran C. J. Brabin and Sons, "The Oldest Firm of Butchers in the City," est. 1848. Young Charles' mother was an invalid, and a rather needy one at that, judging from existing family papers. The Brabin children — Charles and his siblings, John, Edward, and Polly — grew up in the lower middle class; never starving, but never secure in their finances.

After attending college at St. Francis Xavier, young Charles sailed for New York, working as a traveling salesman and hotel clerk. He drifted into the theater, stage managing and acting for two years in *The College Widow*. In 1908 he began acting and directing for Thomas Edison's film company. His family was more than delighted with Charles' success. In a letter home, Brabin begged his father, "there are quite a number of people within the last year who have called on me and who say that you requested them to do so. . . . Most of them were stewards and actors from the incoming vessels who invariably ended up by wanting a position. Now, Dad, you know very well I am not given to false pride, but I do wish you would not request strangers to call upon me here."

By the time he arrived at Fox, Brabin had worked at Vitagraph, Essanay, and Metro; he had also acquired a wife, though he was single again when he met Theda in 1919.

Theda, of course, was the most eligible single woman in Hollywood, and she was immediately smitten by her new director. "His mental brilliance was not the first attractive quality I noticed about him," she reminisced decades later. "It was the way he walked. Like an Indian. Or, as if he wore seven-league boots. He stalked in and in two strides crossed the room. It still fascinates me to sit and watch him approach me."

The obvious electricity on the set between star and director was a promising start for *Kathleen Mavourneen*; the script and extra money donated by Fox kept everyone's hopes up. The money provided for an Irish village set, complete not only with the castle of the villain, but also the quaint though dirt-poor homes of Kathleen and her beloved. Theda, decked out in the simplest cotton frocks that George Hopkins could come up with, cavorted with pigs and chickens, danced jigs, and strolled through fields of flowers, the carefully filtered sunlight making her look years younger.

Vamp: The Rise and Fall of Theda Bara

Advance word in the press perked up interest in the film community and in fan magazines. Despite her recent poor films, the fan mail and gifts continued to pour in — 1,186 pounds of mail and one hundred pounds of candy a month (the latter donated to hospitals — one can only hope that none of it had been poisoned). Hopeful writers sent their ideas; hopeful stars sent photos. One Fox release claimed that Theda received 1,329 marriage offers, though that should be viewed with some suspicion. Some of the gifts were rather alarming: an amateur archeologist from Auburn, New York, sent Theda some old bones (including a skull) and jewelry he had dug up in an Indian village, and some British officers in India shipped her the skin of a 10' 6" tiger they'd shot. Significantly, she also received a shawl from an Irish fan; Theda looked upon this as a good omen.

Filming on *Kathleen Mavourneen* wrapped around the 4th of July, and release was planned for early August. Theda, extremely sure of herself, gave Fox one last chance to hold onto her; she asked that her salary of $4000 a week be increased to $5000. Fox turned her down flat, although he did offer her the chance to do some location films in Europe. Theda, sure that *Kathleen* would be her ticket to a better contract at another studio, refused.

In a rather petty move, Fox planted an item in the press that Theda had walked out on the filming of *Kathleen Mavourneen* and refused to return until her supposed $1500 a week salary had been increased to $4000, and that she now wanted a further $1000 a week. Actually, Theda had been getting yearly increases in her paycheck as a matter of course, and had only requested that she be given an early raise before her contract came up for renewal.

As the summer of 1919 wore on, both Theda and Fox were strongly hinting to the press that their association would come to an end when Theda's five-year contract expired that fall. Fox assigned her two more run-of-the-mill programmers. She would

A coy Fleurette with her husband (Warburton Gamble) in *La Belle Russe* (1919). *Photo: The Everett Collection.*

spend the rest of her contract, August and September 1919, "slinking and writhing and wriggling her eyes."

As *Kathleen Mavourneen* was being edited for release, Theda began filming *La Belle Russe*. It was the old good twin/bad twin fable, in this case based on a stage play which had starred Rose Coghlan back in 1882. As Fleurette, the good sister, Theda played a ballet star who marries a poor but honest military man. As the evil twin, La Belle Russe, Theda tries to steal Fleurette's husband.

A particularly hilarious promotional still for *La Belle Russe*. Photo: *The Everett Collection*.

Theda felt as though she were re-making her second film, *The Kreutzer Sonata*, only with herself playing both sisters.

Filming a dual role could sometimes be artistically satisfying, but was physically punishing, as Florence LaBadie noted in a 1916 interview. The energetic and sturdy actress called the work "exhausting and wearing. A double exposure picture tests the actress as nothing else in pictures."

Theda didn't mind hard work if her heart was in it, but *La Belle Russe* was a dreadful film, and she looked overweight and silly in her tutu. She knew her time at Fox was up, but at least hoped to finish her contract with some decent films. Only the fact that Charles Brabin was guiding her through *La Belle Russe* kept Theda relatively content.

Kathleen Mavourneen opened on August 19. Advance word was promising, raising Theda's hopes: Louella Parsons called it "one of the best performances of her career." *The Houston Chronicle* said that "Miss Bara has a happy part and plays it with great feeling. Her role as Kathleen is a new one to her, but one which she invests with both beauty and charm."

Then all hell broke loose. The Friends of Irish Freedom and The Central Council of Irish Associations violently objected to the depiction of poverty in Ireland (although castles and middle class towns were also shown). Other groups — in a foreshadowing of today's Politically Correct casting furor — objected to a "Jewess" portraying a beloved Irish heroine. Stink bombs were rolled down the aisles in theaters playing *Kathleen.*

In San Francisco, two Catholic priests protested the film and demanded that cuts be made; theater manager Matkowitz agreed and showed the censored version. It did no good: crowds rioted, causing $3,000 worth of damage and injuring several women. Matkowitz pulled *Kathleen Mavourneen* and substituted another film for the duration of the run.

The same thing happened across the country: protests spread and violence broke out in theater after theater. Riot police were called out in several instances; projectors were smashed, film reels stolen. Death threats were phoned and mailed to Fox, Theda, and theater owners. Despite the good reviews, *Kathleen Mavourneen* was yanked hastily from theaters after a day or two; many simply refused the film and sent it back to the distributors unopened. The film that was supposed to be Theda's ticket to a better studio turned out to be the biggest theatrical disaster within memory.

When *La Belle Russe* was released in late September, the notices were much what Theda had anticipated: "The vehicle is not subtle, nor are the machinations of the star. She still pursues the `walk right up and knock 'em down' method that automatically elected her queen of the vamps." W. K. Hollander agreed that "the story is trite and is acted theatrically by players who for the most part are stilted and artificial." Hollander went so far as to take Theda to task for her "large staring eyes and distorted mouth," which made her look "grewsome."

Theda felt beaten and defeated. Only the encouragement of her family and her new-found closeness to Charles Brabin kept her spirits up. She began filming her last Fox project, *The Lure of Ambition*, just after the *Kathleen* debacle, and it was all Theda could do to drag herself to the studio in disgrace day after day. To make matters worse, Brabin was pulled from this film and replaced with Edmund Lawrence. Theda saw this as a final slap in the face from William Fox and could hardly bring herself to utter his name without flinching.

Depressing her even further was the fact that Theda's pet dog came to a horrible end that same month. Her maid took the dog for a walk, and it dashed off the leash, galloping into some hot asphalt being laid by road workers. The animal was so badly burned it had to be destroyed, much to Theda's grief.

Theda, as one newspaper put it, had "more trouble with her pet dogs than a Wall Street broker would have in a Bolshevist meeting." The dog which died in 1919 was Theda's seventh: all had come to unhappy ends via cars, distemper, or other dogs. Theda's

Theda with Belva, her most famous dog. *Photo: The Everett Collection.*

mother recalled that even as a child, her pet dog Sport had expired under Theda's chair, causing no end of hysteria. Her most famous dog was Belva, a photogenic white Russian wolfhound, who died in 1917. A *Photoplay* reporter showed up for a story and photo shoot one day and was distraught to hear of Belva's recent death. Theda, making the best of a bad situation, insisted she communicated with Belva through her crystal ball.

When the reporter told her he couldn't hear a thing, Theda raised one eyebrow meaningfully and snapped, "Well, if you didn't hear it, you can't write a story, can you? Now listen again." The reporter finally caught on and went back to the office to compose his story, "Ghostly Belva Barks at Theda."

Though Theda made light of Belva's death, her mother was quick to add a postscript. Belva had died on Theda's birthday, said Pauline, and "she sat up the night thru, giving him his medicine at fifteen-minute intervals, vainly trying to save his life."

Theda's swan song for the studio that made her a star was a silly tale of a social-climbing British vamp who becomes the Duchess of Rutledge by driving the Duke's current wife to an early grave. When *The Lure of Ambition* was released on November 16, it was not accompanied by the circus sideshow of press hand-outs, goofy exhibitor's promos, or wacky newspaper plants that were the hallmark of Theda's earlier films. *The Lure of Ambition* fairly sneaked in and out of theaters. It was not widely reviewed — but Theda herself got good notices. "Theda does some wonderful things in this flickering fillum," said *The Blade* of Toledo, one of the few papers to give it space, "and we caught ourselves holding our breath every once in a while."

By the time that review hit the stands, Theda had packed up

her personal articles and left Fox Studios for the last time. Too depressed to go job-hunting, she took off on a European cruise with Lori. She only saw William Fox once more, on a Chicago street in the 1920's. The two passed each other by without a word.

J. Gordon Edwards personally chose actress Betty Blythe to succeed Theda as Fox studio's next vamp, starring her in *The Queen of Sheba* (1921). Blythe exclaimed that "I wear 28 costumes, and if I put them all on at once, I couldn't keep warm." Blythe had a respectable but unremarkable career; after a brief vogue in the 1920's, she stayed on-screen through the '40's. Fox re-made *A Fool There Was* in 1922, starring Estelle Taylor. It bombed; Theda gleefully saved the notices.

William Fox did not enjoy very good fortune after Theda left his stables, though the 1920's were a flush time for him: he began experimenting with talking pictures in 1922, introducing Fox Movietone News in 1927. He publicly took on Henry Ford for his anti-Semitism, and was in the process of buying up controlling interest in Loew's when the stock market crashed in 1929. From there on it was all downhill. He had to sell not only his Loew's stock but also controlling interest in the studio that bore his own name. He declared bankruptcy in 1936 and served six months in jail in 1941 for attempting to bribe a Federal judge. After his release, Fox tried to start up in business again, but no one in Hollywood would return his calls, and he sank into obscurity. By the time of his death in 1952, William Fox was as distant a figure from the past as Theda Bara.

Theda returned to New York from her European jaunt, settled back into her West End Avenue apartment and began giving the bluntest interviews of her life. She told Alvin R. Plough that she'd

Vamp: The Rise and Fall of Theda Bara

left Fox because "my health was bad and I needed a rest. I had been getting wretched stories. Very little is expected of a vampire beyond exposing the skin and rolling the eyes. If she can register horror it is quite an asset. The work jarred terribly upon me at first. It was so foreign that I came to hate everything and everyone connected with it. I began to fear I would never like anyone I met again. Looking back, now, I feel I considered myself too high for the movies. Being a vampire is a great hardship. I cannot go anywhere without being pointed at or having a crowd following me. Mother and sister have refused to accompany me on shopping tours. I am afraid that I am exceptionally prim in my ideas and in my private life . . ."

Throwing caution to the winds, she even bad-mouthed some of her own performances. "Have you ever met a woman who hunched her shoulder and looked sidewise at a man to attract him?" she asked. "I haven't, although I may have done it on the screen. Why did I do it? Because people prefer an exaggerated fiction to a subtle fact and because it is much easier to project the obvious than the profound."

When an interviewer asked her if she might retire, Theda said, "After all I have been through, do you think that I would give up now?" She put a good face on her situation and chirpily told the reporter that "since I made my last picture I have been having the time of my life. I feel just like a little child on a picnic, for we all motor out into the country and have our lunch in the open air and sunshine."

Faux-Russian actress Olga Petrova (nee Muriel Harding), another waning vamp, interviewed Theda for *Shadowland* in 1920. She sneeringly described Theda as "a little blue mouse whose gentle ears I hesitated to shock with even an allusion to anyone so fantastically sinful as the screen would have us believe Theda's heroines to be."

The ladies matched wits over tea. When Petrova tried to flaunt her own learning, Theda settled her hash by accurately quoting Nietzsche in German. When Petrova asked, "why did you leave Fox?" Theda sweetly countered, "Why did *you* leave Metro?"

For all her cheerful talk and bantering quips, Theda knew she was fighting for her life. For the first time in five years, she was out of work and her career was in ruins.

Chapter 9

The Unchastened Woman

O ne of the first things Theda did when she was free of her Fox contract was to unload the ludicrous vamp abode she'd been living in since her 1917 arrival in California. Her old-money neighbors on West Adams Boulevard breathed a sigh of relief to see the snake-handling publicity magnet pack up and leave. They were hardly amused when the house was bought — for $250,000 — by Roscoe "Fatty" Arbuckle, the childlike slapstick comic. Arbuckle and his occasional roommate, Buster Keaton, promptly began throwing loud boisterous parties, fueled by their fully stocked wine cellar, carefully hidden from Prohibition agents.

Arbuckle managed to hold onto the West Adams Boulevard house during his manslaughter trial and acquittal in 1921 and 1922. In 1923 he rented the house to Theda's former director Raoul Walsh and Miriam Cooper (who was, for the time being, Mrs. Walsh). The following year Norma Talmadge and her husband Joseph Schenck moved in; eventually, the house became a home for Catholic priests. Six-forty-nine West Adams Boulevard still stands today in West Los Angeles. It was one of the few homes on the block left untouched by the 1992 riots.

Theda went shopping around at other studios, but they refused to see her as anything but a vamp; and who, in 1920, wanted a vamp? At the age of thirty-five — looking slimmer and more beautiful than she had in years — Theda found herself a has-been.

Left: Portrait still, early 1920's. *Photo: Arbe Bareis.*

A possible rescuer came in the form of Broadway entrepreneur A. H. Woods. He approached Theda with a play called *The Lost Soul* (later retitled *The Blue Flame*). Theda should have known what she was in for: in his 1951 obituary, Woods was described by *Variety* as "Producer of Hokey Hits and Flops." A Runyonesque character who never took himself — or his profession — too seriously, Al Woods made his name producing such lurid Bowery melodramas as *Queen of the White Slaves* and *Bertha the Sewing Machine Girl*, as well as promoting prize-fighters and bridge-jumpers. By the time he approached Theda, Woods was also producing respectable Broadway shows, but the air of the Bowery still clung to him.

The major mystery of Theda Bara's career is what could have possessed her to appear in this play. Even after five years at Fox, it's hard to believe she could have drummed up much enthusiasm for *The Blue Flame* on its own merits. Only a combination of desperation and incredibly poor judgement could excuse her signing on for the project; it was far, far worse than any film ever handed her.

The Blue Flame told the story of Ruth Gordon (an odd choice of name, as actress Ruth Gordon was already well known) and her agnostic fiancé, scientist John Varnum. Varnum has invented a device to bring the dead back to life and gets to test it out when pious, sweet-natured Ruth is fortuitously struck down by lightning. Ruth, of course, reawakens as a soulless vampire, giving Theda a field day: rather than "where am I?" her first words are, "Kiss me, dearie!" The plot gets worse and worse; according to one account, "Ruth seduces nice young men. Ruth murders one of them. Ruth drives another down to Chinatown a dope fiend. Ruth is the cause of the death of his fiancée. Ruth — as [columnist] F. P. A. made so bold to declare last night — is stranger than fiction." Just when it seems the play cannot possibly get any worse, it all turns out to have been Varnum's dream. His Ruth is the sweet girl of old, and the newly religious scientist smashes his infernal machine.

Portrait stills from *The Blue Flame* (1920). *Photos: The Everett Collection.*

Theda herself seemed to profess a clear-eyed and prescient view of the proceeding, telling reporter Karl Kitchen, "It's not a great drama, is it? But it will make a beautiful film play my 10 and 15 cent public will adore." She had three or four scripts to choose from, Theda said. "I knew that some people wanted to see me as a good little girl and that some other people wanted to see me as a bad little girl. *The Blue Flame* gave me both roles."

No less than two directors (J. C. Huffman and W. H. Gilmore) were hired to shepherd Theda through the show; the supporting cast included the talented Allen Dinehart. Theda started rehearsals in January 1920, and *The Blue Flame* had out-of-town tryouts in Pittsburgh, Washington, Stamford, and Chicago in February. Business was amazing; records were broken in all four cities, crowds packed the alleyways and streets surrounding the theaters. The newspapers were so stunned by Theda's reception that no one paid much attention to the play; Broadway-bound shows always underwent a lot of revision on the road, anyway.

The March 1 opening in Boston was literally a riot. The Majestic Theater was packed to the rafters, and such a crowd gathered outside that police had to be called in. Woods — ever the showman — had arranged for "fourteen milk white horses" to deliver Theda back to her hotel, but she sensibly rebelled and opted for a limousine (hysterical fans held onto the running boards as long as they could). Theda played Boston for two weeks — including extra matinees — and the show sold out.

Then, on March 15, *The Blue Flame* hit Broadway.

The Shubert Theater, on Broadway and 44th Street, was packed with Theda's family, hard-bitten New York critics, celebrities (including Mae Murray, Geraldine Farrar, Florence Reed, Lewis Selznick, Norma Talmadge and Theda's little Fox co-stars Jane and Katherine Lee). Mostly, the house was crowded with lucky film fans anxious to see their idol in person.

Theda knew her opening night was a disaster. She had a bad cold and, she recalled, "my voice was tight and I felt as though I couldn't make a sound. Someone told me to go out and apologize for my voice. But I wouldn't. I suppose my fighting blood was up. Many of those in the audience were people who hated me. And I wouldn't go out and apologize to them." She also suffered an embarrassing mishap onstage. During her death scene, "my leading man picked me up and threw me down on the couch so that my skirts went up to my knees. My first impulse was to sit up and pull them down. Fortunately, I remembered that I was dead. And so I lay there and said to myself, `Now everyone is saying that I want to show my legs'."

That was the least of what everyone was saying; the reviews were nothing less than vicious. "At the end of the third act," wrote Heywood Broun, "she made a speech in which she said that God had been very kind to her. Probably she referred to the fact that at no time during the course of the evening did the earth open and swallow up the authors, the star, and all the company."

The only question was, which was worse: the play or Theda's performance? The nicest things anyone could say about Theda was that "she is an actress of average competence," "Miss Bara is not so bad," and "satisfactory enough." "You can hear every word she says," offered one paper lamely. Nearly everyone mentioned how lovely she looked, much younger and slimmer than on film; her costumes by W. M. de Lignemare got the only good notices of the show.

Others were not so kind. "To see a crude actress, no matter how famous she is in the films," said Louis Reed in *The Dramatic Mirror*, "unfamiliar with the rudiments of dramatic art . . . strutting about extravagantly in a series of maudlin episodes is not really worth fifteen minutes time." "Variety is utterly absent, nor is there a trace of emotion," said a stringer from Kansas City. "She had a school-girl's recitif, a western monotony, and a sort of black alpaca dreariness," added Alan Dale of *The New York American*.

But Theda's personal notices sounded like love letters compared to what critics unleashed upon *The Blue Flame* itself. The only saving grace was that the play was bad enough to be funny, as Alexander Woollcott noted. "You know how it is when you have visitors from out of town and possessed to go on a perfectly delightful slumming party down on the Bowery or somewhere to see one of those killing melodramas — oh come on, won't it be fun? . . . Well, *The Blue Flame* is the kind of play you always expect the cheap theatres to show, and they never do." Louis Reed called it "the most terrible play within the memory of the writer . . . one of those rare occasions when a play is so hopeless that it is funny." *The New York Post* agreed: "it was received with derisive laughter by the curious audience."

Even the special effects were derided. One critic noted that

Vamp: The Rise and Fall of Theda Bara

Ruth's soul, when it ascended to the theater's rafters, looked like nothing so much as a large molar.

Lines like, "I'll shake you like I shake my shimmy!" "Did you bring the cocaine?" and "You make my heart laugh and I feel like a woman of the streets" brought down the house. It must have taken every ounce of Theda's professionalism to go on, but she brazened it through. "I really don't know what the critics said about me," she sniffed the next day. "I haven't read them at all. They might disturb me if I did."

Not only did *The Blue Flame* not close, but it played to packed houses for two months before going out on tour. "Since Miss Bara opened at the Shubert Theater," one paper noted with amazement, "there have been larger crowds at the stage door of that house than have ever been known before in its history." People came to see Theda; they came to laugh; they came because it was the camp thing to do. But, in short, they came. Theda was earning not only a regular salary of $1500 a week, but had a fifty-percent interest in the play. Her two weeks in Boston alone had added $11,000 to her bank account. Weekly receipts in New York averaged $15,000. *The Blue Flame* made Theda a very wealthy woman.

It also made her a laughingstock, ruining any chance for a serious acting career. There is no getting around the fact that she was just plain awful in *The Blue Flame*, and it cannot be laid simply to bad writing. Whatever talent, whatever spark Theda possessed on-screen just didn't translate over the footlights. Her lack of success from 1905 to 1914 becomes less mysterious in view of her performance as Ruth Gordon. Theda Bara was — arguably — a brilliant and talented film actress. But as a stage star, she was hopeless.

Theda agreed to tour in *The Blue Flame* through 1920. "I am going to stay on the stage and I am going to make pictures, too," she defiantly told one reporter. She did take a midsummer vacation, sailing to France with her sister to go clothes-shopping. Lori had a much better time than Theda; she met *New York Tribune* reporter Frank Getty on shipboard and married him in London. Lori came home with Theda to break the news to mother; the Gettys eventually settled in France. Theda didn't even find any clothes to her liking in Paris, coming home with a starry-eyed new-lywed sister and a shipment of empty trunks. The only fun she had was appearing in a shipboard production. The parody melodrama, *The Deadly Secret, or Love Triumphant*, was performed by passengers under the auspices of "The Migratory Stock Company." Theda saved the program, but happily, no reviewers were on board. She had enough of those waiting for her on dry land.

Theda returned to the States in late August to finish her *Blue Flame* tour, finally closing the show on January 1, 1921. Even without Fox's help, Theda's vampire reputation still hounded her. While back in Boston with *The Blue Flame* in September, Theda and her maid found themselves on an elevator with a young married couple. The wife suddenly recognized the famed man-trap, and "it was perfectly evident what was going on in her mind. The elevator had barely stopped when she took the man by the arms and liter-ally pushed him out of the door ahead of her!" Theda turned to her maid and laughed, "Well — she must have thought I was a quick worker!"

Reporters found her to be the same dull homebody. "I read, and take the dogs for a walk," she told *The American Magazine* that same month. "I don't do anything very exciting. I don't go in for sports. I'm not in the least athletic. In fact, I'm afraid I'm a physical coward. I don't like to be hurt."

She was finally free from the shackles of Fox and able to express her own opinions in her own words. Those words sound more like a Rhodes Scholar than a movie star; Theda's education and reading gave her a vocabulary and phrasing which sound impossibly stilted today. "The first impression Theda Bara made on me," said one reporter, "was that of a remarkable and burning intellectuality. Her English is as crystalline as [British stage actress]

Phyllis Neilson-Terry's, and she uses the ranging vocabulary of a literary man."

Claiming to have discovered a nascent feminism, Theda said at this time that "I am the champion of women. I do not think that men have ever treated our sex fairly, even Nature has been against us from the start and is against us today. The woman always gets the worst of it from man, and always will, for this reason."

With *The Blue Flame* finally over and done with, Theda signed with Marcus Loew for a vaudeville tour. Unfortunately, she couldn't actually *do* anything: Theda was not a singer, dancer or comedienne. But just her appearance was enough. Audiences paid good money, happily, for a chance to hear Theda chat about her career, about women, sex and vampires. Then she took a few questions from the audience. It was not unlike the "Evening with . . ." series which Bette Davis, Joan Crawford, and others made so popular in the 1970's. At the end of her speech, she asked the audience, "will you all wish me to play the vampire again?" to raucous applause. When she continued, "would you also like to see me in the role of a good girl?" the response was muted. "Well, there you are . . ." she sighed.

The high point of the tour came in Tulsa, where brother Marque was working for Bell Oil. His co-workers had no idea he was related to the famous star, and he got no end of kidding when Theda and her entourage descended on him for a week. She played on the same bill as Evangelist Billy Sunday; he and Theda chatted civilly for reporters and broke all box office records.

Theda made yet another fortune in vaudeville, but something was lacking. She hated hotels, missed her mother and sister, and suddenly found herself missing Charles Brabin more and more. She returned to New York in the spring of 1921; Brabin was working on the East Coast and the two began seeing more of each other.

Going all girlish, she told a reporter what happened next. "And then — and then, oh, you know how those things, go, don't

Pauline Goodman *(right)* admires her daughters Lori *(left)* and Theda in 1920. *Photo: Motion Picture Classic, Chester Clarke.*

you? I began to get interested in him, and he took me out to lunch, and we had some long interesting talks, and he came to my house to see my mother, and — well, I became engaged."

The two planned to drive up to Connecticut in mid-June to tie the knot. "Neither of us had ever been on time in our lives," she recalled, years later. "So I thought, `I'll shampoo my hair.' And then bless you if the man wasn't actually punctual. I had to stick up my wet hair under my picture hat, and sneezed throughout the ceremony."

Exactly where and when the ceremony took place was kept a deep secret; the wedding was never actually announced, and it was months before the Brabins would admit to the press that they were indeed married. They took off for a honeymoon in Nova Scotia, where Charles owned a thousand-acre estate. "There are six farms on it," Charles wrote to his father, "and about one million and a quarter feet of lumber. Some day, if I ever have enough money, I shall build up there. For the present I have a bungalow that is rather cozy." One reporter who tracked them down wrote that "Mr. and Mrs. Brabin swam and fished and went boating like any two young people in the woods." The Brabins returned from their honeymoon to New York and moved temporarily into Theda's West End Avenue apartment.

Theda fulfilled the rest of her vaudeville tour, but at Charles' request, did not sign up for another season. By the time Theda married Charles Brabin, she had been a working woman for more than a decade, the main support of her family for five years. Before that, she'd been an independent, modern college girl. Suddenly she was whisked back to Victorian days, married to an old-fashioned husband. When asked years later why she'd retired, she sighed, "I married an Englishman — need I say more?"

Charles Brabin's mother had been an invalid; his sister stayed home and had children. Brabin women did not work, and people who knew Theda and Charles had their doubts as to the marriage's viability. Theda still had ambitions both for stage and screen; Charles was a successful director with no patience or real respect for his wife's career. His attitude — a mixture of dismay and pride — comes through in a letter to his father, written shortly after their marriage:

> Last Saturday my wife was due to open in Atlantic City at 7 o'clock that evening. We were unfortunate enough to miss the train, but by chartering a hydroplane we made the trip of 120 miles in 58 minutes. I enclose you a snap taken of our arrival and in the presence of some 10,000 people. I have a dis-

Charles and Theda Brabin on one of their many cross-country jaunts, in 1923. *Photo: The Everett Collection.*

taste for the crowd and the newspapers and from now on Mrs. Brabin must run the gauntlet alone.

Running the gauntlet alone was what saved the Bara-Brabin marriage. The two were grown adults, set in their ways, and were smart enough to give each other a free rein. Theda rarely visited Charles' film sets; both traveled separately, Theda often accompanied by her mother or sister. These separations — though occasionally provoking divorce rumors in the press — actually kept the Brabins' marriage fresh and strong. When Theda tired of her peremptory husband, or Charles of his ambitious wife, one of them simply took off for a month or two and returned happy and calmed. This method worked for more than thirty years.

But still, Theda clung to the hope that her film career might somehow be revived. Newspapers announced her return to the screen in 1922, when Selznick Pictures Corporation was said to have signed her for one film. Twenty-year-old David O. Selznick was courting Theda, having just entered the production business through his father, Lewis. She was by no means a has-been at the time, and there was much interest in the project; letters poured in to Theda, Selznick and even Fox. That same year, Theda was named one of the screen's twelve most beautiful actresses, although she had not appeared in a movie for three years. The fact that the judge was David O. Selznick didn't escape anyone's notice.

"I've been reading submitted manuscripts steadily for weeks," Theda told *Motion Picture*, "and have come across nothing suitable yet. And unfortunately, good stories don't always mean good screen stories. The novels I enjoy most are wholly unadaptable for screen use because they are generally straight psychology and no action." She never found a story, and her Selznick contract lapsed.

She and Charles, on one of their trips to his Nova Scotia estate, discussed filming *Evangeline* on location. Dolores Del Rio eventually made the film in 1929, but the Bara/Brabin version never materialized.

In September 1923, Charles was shipped off to Italy by Metro's Louis B. Mayer to direct their epic *Ben-Hur*, starring George Walsh. Things, to put it mildly, did not go well. Brabin was to spend a year and a half struggling to get the huge, unwieldy film under control.

Meanwhile, back in the U. S., more Theda Bara comeback rumors surfaced. In 1924, it was announced in *Movie Weekly* that she had formed Theda Bara Productions, and was about to film the society drama *Déclassé*, which Ethel Barrymore had played onstage. Another five to eight films would be made through 1926, said the article. But nothing ever came of it.

Something did come of another offer, from a small, struggling studio called Chadwick (their slogan, "Every Picture an Achievement," could be taken in more than one way). They approached

214

Theda visits Mary Pickford on the set of *Rosita* (1923); Theda and Charles Brabin at a party in the 1920's. *Photos: New York Public Library for the Performing Arts.*

Theda in late 1924 with *The Unchastened Woman*, which had been a minor Broadway hit for Emily Stevens ten years earlier.

In this comedy/drama, Theda played Caroline Knollys, a newly pregnant society wife who discovers her husband is cheating on her. Caroline takes off for Europe, has her baby and becomes "The toast of Venice . . . The most talked about woman in Europe," a title she apparently assumes by having tea with middle-aged gentlemen. She returns home, simultaneously scandalizing and titillating her husband by "playing flame to the moths who have fluttered after her from Europe." Eventually she takes back her grovelling husband and all ends happily. "All men are simply children," Caroline sighs, "and I guess I can take care of both my boys."

When Theda returned to work in 1925, she was entering an industry that had completely re-invented itself. Although some of the old guard (Fairbanks, Pickford, Gish, Chaplin, Swanson) were as popular as ever, much had changed. Some of the biggest, most exciting stars of 1925 had been insignificant small-timers when Theda had vanished from the screen: John Gilbert, Mae Murray, Harold Lloyd, Rudolph Valentino, Lon Chaney. Younger vamps such as Pola Negri and Nita Naldi had succeeded her. But more important, and more ominous for Theda, were the flappers.

These jazzy, ultra-modern girls were a whole new breed. Most were young enough to be Theda's daughters, and looked it. The matronly, adult sophistication popular in the 1910's was a thing of the past. Colleen Moore, Joan Crawford, and, most of all, Clara Bow, made it impossible for the forty-year-old Theda to regain her status as a sex symbol. Some of her contemporaries, like Alice Joyce and Kathlyn Williams, were easing into character roles. Others, like Pearl White and Blanche Sweet, faded slowly but gracefully from view.

Not only stars, but also films, had changed. "Super-Extravaganzas" like *Cleopatra* now looked rather quaint. Acting styles had shifted to a quieter, more natural tone; camera work, lighting, and makeup had improved with the years. Theda had attended openings of many landmark films during her five-year retirement: *The Cabinet of Dr. Caligari*, Nazimova's brilliant financial flop *Salome*, *Orphans of the Storm, The Covered Wagon, Safety Last, Greed, The Thief of Bagdad* — all outstripping anything Fox had given Theda. Even the biggest, most sophisticated of her films now seemed laughably old-fashioned.

So, sadly, did *The Unchastened Woman*. That same year, another film was made with a similar plot but a very different sensibility. In *Dancing Mothers*, Alice Joyce played the put-upon wife who leaves her husband and daughter (Clara Bow, in a break-through part). But unlike Theda's character, Alice Joyce stands by her decision to leave when her selfish family begs her to return. *Dancing Mothers* was firmly planted in the 1920's; *The Unchastened Woman* still had the lingering morality of the Victorian age about it.

Left: Theda with John Miljan in *The Unchastened Woman* (1925). *Photo: Robert S. Birchard. Right:* Portrait still from *The Unchastened Woman. Photo: Archive Photos.*

Seen today, though, *The Unchastened Woman* is a surprisingly enjoyable film, mixing marital melodrama with light, wry comedy. It's dated, of course, but the plot moves along at a nice clip and the performances hold up quite well. Theda excels in scenes where she bitchily puts down her husband and his girlfriend, showing an unexpected flair for light comedy. She looks lovely: her face was fuller and her makeup expertly applied, giving Theda a more youthful, softer appearance than she'd had at the height of her career.

Chadwick certainly didn't stint on sets and costumes, perhaps renting them from one of the major studios. The Knollys mansion and the scenes of Venice are as lush and well-appointed as anything M-G-M might have come up with. The lighting and camera work are a bit flat (though it's hard to judge fairly, considering how faded existing prints are). Theda is decked out in a flattering series of flowing tea dresses and evening gowns, her hair done up in pearls.

217

The film, however, got lukewarm reviews upon its release late in 1925. Sally Benson summed up the general opinion of *The Unchastened Woman* when she wrote, "when I realized that this was Theda Bara's comeback picture, and not just one of her old releases, I could hardly believe my eyes."

In early 1925, Theda's very chastened husband returned from Italy, having been unceremoniously booted off *Ben-Hur*. When Metro merged with Goldwyn, Marcus Loew took one look at the financial disaster brewing in Italy and sailed over there post-haste with replacement director Fred Niblo and replacement star Ramon Novarro. *Ben-Hur*, when it was finally released in 1926, was one of the best films of the year. It's still an impressive achievement, but nothing of Brabin's work remains in the final release.

Brabin had been a bit taken aback when Theda wrote to him about her plans to film *The Unchastened Woman*; she never would have had the nerve to do another film against his wishes had he not been half a world away. When he came back to hearth and home, Brabin had a bigger shock awaiting him: Theda had entered negotiations with Hal Roach to do a series of comedy shorts. Brabin's reaction can only be imagined.

In November, 1925, Theda traveled to New York, where she announced to reporters that she'd signed on with Roach to do the shorts. "Vamping requires no artistry whatsoever," she sniffed. "High comedy, I believe, is the best test of an actress' ability. It is the most difficult thing in the world. But somehow it sweeps you along, carries you like a wave carries a swimmer." While she was at it, Theda got in a slam at California: "I am going to New York now to wake myself up. I have been in California so long that I feel like I am just coming out of a long sleep."

If Theda wanted to do "high comedy," the Roach lot was the

wrong place to look for it. Roach was Mack Sennett's successor in the field of knock-about two-reel comedies. His "Lot of Fun," as it was called, produced the famed Our Gang shorts, as well as early comedies of Harold Lloyd, Charley Chase and Harry Langdon. In 1926 he teamed contract players Stan Laurel and Oliver Hardy; Roach went on to help launch the careers of Jean Harlow, Thelma Todd, and Janet Gaynor.

In late 1925, Roach was trying to improve the public image of his films and started an "All-Star" company. "We are negotiating with every big name in the business that is not under contract to appear with or support our comedians," he told a Philadelphia distributor. By that fall he had signed Theda, Lionel Barrymore, and Glenn Tryon (Roach wooed Theda with flowers and sweet-talk).

The first of Theda's shorts for Roach was called *High Explosive* (later changed to *Madame Mystery* to avoid competing with a similarly named book). It was filmed from December 10th through 24th, 1925. Theda worked seven days a week, but was well paid: She made a total of $15,000 for that one little film. It was co-directed by Stan Laurel and featured his future partner Oliver Hardy in a bit part as a ship's captain. *Madame Mystery*, which still exists in a shortened form, is a very odd and rather grisly little film.

Theda — looking lovely in some surprisingly chic costumes for a two-reeler — plays the title role, a woman "whose secret activities have baffled the keenest minds of all Europe." Most of the action takes place on an ocean liner, where two bungling thieves and a spy try to steal Madame's cargo, a "helium nitrate" bomb. One of the thieves accidentally swallows it, to everyone's alarm. The "bomb" turns out to be non-explosive helium, which expands hideously, causing the thief (with his partner clinging to his pants leg) to float away. In a particularly unpleasant ending, a pelican pecks the poor man's stomach and he explodes.

Theda threw herself into the spirit of the film, overacting her head off: she flings her arms about, does quite decent double-takes

Madame Mystery poster art, 1926. *Photo: The Everett Collection.*

and glares haughtily in a Margaret Dumont manner. Hal Roach was anxious to have her continue the series, but Theda was a bit discouraged by the results and was secretly relieved when Charles forbade her. The contract was cancelled.

Madame Mystery was hardly a fitting swan song for her brilliant career, but other stars fared as badly. Garbo's career ended with the dismal *Two Faced Woman,* Joan Crawford's with *Trog,* Mae West's with *Sextette* and Bette Davis' with *The Wicked Stepmother.* Few have the good luck (or good sense) to exit on such a high note as Lillian Gish's *The Whales of August* or Henry Fonda's *On Golden Pond.*

The same year that Theda appeared in *Madame Mystery,* a new vamp appeared in Hollywood. In retrospect, the careers of Theda Bara and Greta Garbo were strikingly similar. Garbo played many

Theater display card from *Madame Mystery*. Theda clings to ship's captain Oliver Hardy. *Photo: The Everett Collection.*

unrepentant sirens, and like Theda, eventually parodied herself as a comic spy (although *Ninotchka* was light years beyond *Madame Mystery*).

Theda might have proudly noted that Garbo never played Shakespeare as she did, but both starred in *Camille,* and many of their roles were carbon copies: a high-placed mistress (Bara's *Madame DuBarry* and Garbo's *Conquest*); a village-bred opera singer (*The Siren's Song* and *The Torrent*); a woman who seduces her husband's boyhood friend (*The Clemenceau Case* and *Flesh and the Devil*); a straying wife and mother who repents too late (*East Lynne* and *Anna Karenina*); a naughty artist's model (*The Forbidden Path* and *Inspiration*); twin sisters vamping a straying husband (*La Belle Russe* and *Two Faced Woman*); and historical queens Cleopatra and Christina.

221

But Theda's day was over and Garbo's just dawning. *Madame Mystery* marked the last time Theda Bara ever appeared on-screen.

Charles Brabin continued his own distinguished career, directing such films as *So Big* (1925), *Stella Maris* (1926), *The Mask of Fu Manchu* and *The Beast of the City* (both M-G-M, 1932). He retired in 1938; by then the Brabins were an extremely wealthy couple. Colleen Moore, whom Charles directed in *So Big*, later said that "he was the director who could get the most out of me. I was fond of him and also fond of Theda . . . who was a very amusing woman. She used to kid about `Theda Bara' all the time and do lovely imitations of `Theda Bara'."

Theda tried to introduce her British-born husband to the delights of a Midwestern small town in the mid-1920's. The Brabins rented a Spanish-style villa at Victory Parkway and Ledgewood in Cincinnati (now part of Xavier University) and for several years used it as their way station between New York and California.

She finally gave up her West End Avenue apartment in New York, but rented another at 14 East 60th Street in a chic district not far from Central Park and the major clothing and book stores. The Brabins purchased a surprisingly small but attractive home in a nice section of Beverly Hills, at 632 North Alpine Drive. The house, half hidden from the street by trees, was comfortable but elegant; the combined art and furnishing collections of Theda and Charles left no doubt that this was a very wealthy couple with excellent, quiet taste.

Slowly, the former workaholic Theda came out of her shell and began to enjoy life in a way she had found impossible when employed at Fox. The woman who had scurried home to read after work, who never set foot inside a nightclub during her career,

The Brabins' living room at 632 North Alpine Drive. *Photo: Arbe Bareis.*

Theda's bedroom, 632 North Alpine Drive. *Photo: Arbe Bareis.*

became a social butterfly and latent comic (one paper called her a "modified Dot Parker, she gives a quippy perk to every party"). Photographers frequently caught Theda and her husband out on the town, or Theda lunching at various country clubs and restaurants with pals. She took up golf, and joined a Hollywood "Girl's Club" that included Colleen Moore, the Talmadge sisters, Bessie Love and writers Adela Rogers St. Johns and Frances Marion.

In 1933 Frederick Collins of *The New Movie Magazine* visited Theda, half-expecting to encounter "a poor, wizened old woman . . . standing on a Hollywood street corner asking for alms." He found, instead, a lovely, youthful society matron with a great sense of perspective. "I am the `forgotten woman' now, you know," she laughed. The two chatted for hours about movies old and new, and about Theda's retirement. Referring to Jean Harlow and Mae West, Theda claimed that "the wickedest thing I ever did on the screen would seem tame now." She reiterated the fact that she left the screen to please her husband. When Collins doubted that a forceful woman like Theda could be so cowed, she leaned forward and confided, "you have no idea! He won't even let me have a dog." Brabin did, incidentally, allow her one Persian cat.

Theda knew all the directors and stars, and saw most of the new movies. In 1934 a United Press reporter spoke with her about the modern vampires of the 1930's. If she felt any pangs of jealousy about the parade passing her by, Theda didn't let on. Indeed, she became something of a den mother to the young stars who were inheriting the Hollywood that Theda had helped to create. "Garbo wins top honors," she said. "Of course, Marlene Dietrich and Katharine Hepburn are distinctive, too, the former for an exotic blonde beauty and Miss Hepburn for a crisp something that is hers alone. Katharine Hepburn always makes me think of the Winged Victory. She goes striding about, armed in youth and strength, utterly invincible. And Mae West — ah, *there* is a vamp!"

Theda had just had her hair bobbed for the first time and

Theda *(right)* out for a stroll with a friend, Mrs. John D. Farrell, in 1935. *Photo: New York Public Library for the Performing Arts.*

looked the very model of the modern housewife as she reminisced. When it was mentioned that Claudette Colbert was about to re-make *Cleopatra*, Theda tried to be diplomatic. "Although at first you don't classify Claudette Colbert as what was once called a `vampire,' I think she will probably give an excellent performance. When I played the part," she continued, quickly dropping Claudette, "I read every book I could find concerning the Egyptian Queen and discovered to my amazement that she was actually a very capable housewife with several children, not especially beau-tiful nor the physically alluring siren handed down by our leg-endary history."

Theda's last professional stage appearance came in May of that same year, when she appeared in a Little Theater production of *Bella Donna*. Theda portrayed a society divorcée approaching middle age; the show had been a great success for Alla Nazimova in 1912, but was a bit dog-eared by 1934. Nonetheless, the five-night engagement at the Hawthorne Theater in Beverly Hills received warmly nostalgic press. The bad taste of *The Blue Flame* had faded somewhat, and people were kind enough to remember Theda's great successes. She "played with admirable restraint and poise," one paper reported, suggesting only that she might have overdone the climactic scene a bit.

The reviewer also noted that when Theda made her entrance, the show was halted by five solid minutes of heartfelt, enthusiastic applause.

Theda was rarely out of the public eye for more than a year or two. In 1936 she appeared on Lux Radio Theater. She reminisced about the silent screen, telling host Woody Van Dyke that "the director guided us with a one-two-three-four, just as a metronome guides a pianist." Theda added that she would be making more radio appearances as well as "motion picture work. I'm considering an offer now, running through scripts and ideas. Oh, I just hope everybody will be as happy about another Theda Bara picture as I am. The public has been very good to me in the past." By that time, Theda had picked up her husband's accent and sounded more British than he did.

That same year she was announced as one of the cast members of Paramount's *Hollywood Boulevard*, a newspaper drama featuring cameos by silent stars Francis X. Bushman, Mae Marsh, Esther Ralston, Betty Compson and others. "With Bara this picture should pack them in the theaters all over the world," said one newspaper. But the film came and went without much comment, and without Theda.

While Theda settled into her life as a society matron, sister Lori's career as a screenwriter was taking off. Divorced from her

Theda (left) with her sister Lori. *Photo: Motion Picture Magazine, Chester Clarke.*

first husband, she married M-G-M comedy writer Ward Wing in Mexico in 1927. Although Lori had become friendly with Norma Talmadge and several other film people through her sister, she'd never succeeded as an actress. After years of appearing in extra and bit parts, she put her writing talent to work. She shrugged off her acting career, claiming that "I never really wanted to act and never liked it, because you've always got to be thinking of how you look." Asked about her sister, Lori said, "now she lives in Beverly Hills and doesn't do anything but have luncheons and dinners and that sort of thing."

In 1933 Lori and Ward Wing traveled to Malaysia for six months, writing and directing *Samarang*, "a romance of pearl diving," with an all-native cast. The Wings planned another two films, but were divorced in 1935. Brother Marque, meanwhile, was making his own tour of the U.S.; by the 1930's he was in Chicago. He finally settled with his wife, Alma, in Newport, Rhode Island.

One of Theda's biggest thrills in the early 1930's was playing hostess for her idol, stage star Mrs. Patrick Campbell. The eccentric, outspoken "Mrs. Pat," then in her seventies, was penniless and trying to make a comeback in films as a character actress. A close friend of George Bernard Shaw, she had originated his *Pygmalion* and had been a stage star since 1893. "What a supreme artist," Theda glowed years later. "There were times when Mrs. Campbell was, shall we put it, naughty? But I really didn't notice. You see, I knew her pain. The unending battle she had fought all her life." When Mrs. Pat died in 1940 in a nursing home in France, Theda wrote to a friend, "she was a great woman. Certainly the greatest I've ever known."

Theda's mother Pauline lived in Beverly Hills near her daughters, while Bernard Bara stayed in the Midwest, vacationing with his wife in California and in Brabin's Nova Scotia home. It was there, at the age of eighty-three, that he died on August 5, 1936.

Theda spent as much time in her New York apartment as in California, telling columnist Louis Sobol in 1936 that she didn't like "the famed Southern California climate a bit, because it gave her trouble with her nerves and made her feel wretched all the time."

Theda and Charles took off for the cooler climate of Europe shortly thereafter on an extended trip, renting a flat in London's Mayfair district and stopping off in Rome in 1938, where they heard Mussolini speak and had an audience with the Pope. In 1939, with war threatening, the Brabins returned to New York. Theda told reporters that she was reading several plays and hoped to be on Broadway next season. She spoke out against Communism, and, laughing about her long absence from her beloved New York, said she found herself "looking, like a rube, at the tall buildings." Theda continued giving interviews and appearing on radio shows (including Ken Murray's in 1939 and Groucho Marx's in 1943, doing comedy sketches).

In 1941, theatrical agent Alan Brock visited Theda at her East 60th Street apartment to discuss possible projects. He remembers

Posing at a press conference on her return from Europe in 1939. *Photo: New York Public Library for the Performing Arts.*

her as a practical and sincere woman, analytical about her career and able to "stand apart from herself, criticizing herself as an actress." "I wanted to play Ibsen, Molière, but Fox wouldn't hear of it," she groused over cocktails. When Brock mentioned an offer to do a stage satire of *A Fool There Was*, Theda sensibly shuddered in horror at the idea, calling it "unthinkable" and "revolting."

There were so many other roles that Theda could have played, however. With her contacts in Hollywood and her fame, she might have had her pick of a number of delectable character parts suitable for a striking middle-aged lady. In the 1930's and 1940's, Theda might have easily played the roles taken by Marie Dressler in *Dinner at Eight*, Constance Collier in *Stage Door*, Barbara O'Neill in *Gone with the Wind*, Judith Anderson in *Rebecca*. In 1949, Billy Wilder cast Mae West and Montgomery Clift in his dark comedy of old Hollywood, *Sunset Boulevard*. For better or worse, that bizarre pairing quickly fell apart, and Wilder approached Mary Pickford and Pola Negri with the starring part. Both turned it down, finding it a little too close to home, and the still young and trim Gloria Swanson accepted, turning in the performance of her career. Amazingly, Theda Bara was never mentioned as a possible Norma Desmond.

During World War II, then in her late fifties, Theda spent her time shuttling back and forth between coasts, visiting with her mother and sister when not with her husband; throwing dinner parties on the West Coast and attending the theater and opera in New York. Her weight continued to roller-coaster up and down as her gourmet cookery became more expert. Her widespread fame as a cook and hostess gave rise to a George Cukor wisecrack. Attending a play with Ethel Barrymore, he watched the star (Tallulah Bankhead in *Reflected Glory*) order a sumptuous meal which had the audience groaning with pleasure. Leaning over to Barrymore, Cukor whispered, "ah — pot luck at Theda Bara's!"

Something had happened to Theda by the 1940's. Perhaps she sensed that Hollywood had passed her by, or maybe her husband and time finally wore down what remained of her ambition. At any rate, she quietly told a reporter, "I'll never return to pictures. I'm not even interested in a plan for going on the stage in some of the roles I played on-screen. I live only 24 hours a day getting such happiness from life as I can. And that," she added firmly, "is a great deal of happiness. Nothing could induce me to interrupt, much less jeopardize it."

Theda also claimed to be writing her autobiography. "One reason I want to write my story is because nobody ever wrote a true word about me. Some of my work had nothing to do with sirens. Somehow everybody seems to have forgotten that I played in *The Two Orphans* and *Under Two Flags* and *Kathleen Mavourneen*."

She was never able to sell, or even serialize, her memoirs (if

At the Universal-International commissary, visiting Tony Curtis and Piper Laurie. The two newcomers were filming *The Prince Who Was a Thief* (1951). *Photo: Everett Collection.*

they ever indeed existed), but got another idea in 1947 when Paramount made a movie of Pearl White's life (the now almost unwatchable *The Perils of Pauline*, with Betty Hutton). In 1949 former songwriter Buddy DeSylva — then Executive Producer at Paramount — bought Theda's life story as a follow-up for Hutton. Hutton turned down the script, titled *The Great Vampire*, and DeSylva died the following year. The film was never made, to the relief of film fans, who generally detest the various travesties committed upon White, Jeanne Eagels, Marilyn Miller, Jean Harlow and others.

Eventually, Carol Channing starred in a Broadway musical called *The Vamp*, very loosely based on Theda's career. It opened and closed like a camera shutter, one of the resounding flops of 1955.

Vamp: The Rise and Fall of Theda Bara

Theda's last professional photo session came in 1951, when John Engstead shot her for a *Harper's Bazaar* article on living legends. "She excused herself to change," said Engstead, "and returned wearing a lace negligee with her long hair hanging loose and seductively around her shoulders." Somewhat startled to see the sixty-six-year-old actress thus decked out, Engstead quickly shot some photos, then talked Theda into a more dignified evening cloak.

The resulting photos were lovely, but Theda blew up when *Harper's* hit the stands, describing Pola Negri as "the first vamp." "*I* was the first vamp of the screen," Theda hollered at Engstead over the phone. "Pola Negri copied *me*. Something has to be done about this. There must be a retraction." Negri herself was irritated to be confused with the much-older Theda. As the women aged, they looked a great deal alike, and Negri found herself denying that she was Theda almost till her own death in 1987.

By the early 1950's, the Brabins settled into a calm and peaceful existence in Beverly Hills. One anonymous neighbor gave this portrait of Theda Bara in her final years, picturing her more like a quintessential sweet auntie than The Devil's Daughter. "She was a lady with graying hair and an odd pallor to her skin . . . . We used to talk over the fence, this ample lady with the sweet face and the kind heart, as I passed her house and she would be working on her little but immaculate garden. She gave two hours every day to baking cookies and had a large earthenware jar to keep them in. The schoolchildren, coming from school, would cut across her garden and if they followed the path and trampled nothing, they got a cookie and a warm smile, each. They never knew who she was, but we two adults used to laugh about the symbol she was in the silent movies. She was probably the kindest woman I ever met and about as evil as a robin or a tame rabbit . . . All I can think about Theda Bara was that she was enormously kind and friendly

232

Theda's last formal portrait, taken in 1951 by John Engstead. *Photo: Motion Picture and Television Photo Archive.*

to the children of that corner of Los Angeles, a sort of angel with fresh cookies and the prettiest flowers in any garden around."

Theda and Charles even managed to keep the romance alive in their marriage. Film historian Dewitt Bodeen saw birthday cards Theda gave her husband inscribed, "To my darling Mouchy-Mou — from your Wiffle Tree," and called Brabin's affections just as "seventeenish."

In one of her last interviews, Theda waxed nostalgic about the silent screen. "To understand those days," she told Hedda Hopper, "you must consider that people believed what they saw on the screen. Nobody had destroyed the great illusion. Now they know it's all make-believe."

She also took the casually dressed stars of the 1950's to task, in an incisive tirade which holds just as true today as it did then. "It's the stars themselves who have been failing the fans. People have always been hungry for glamour — they still are. But it takes showmanship and a constant sense of responsibility to hold their interest. A star mustn't allow her public to see her in slacks. She should dress beautifully at all times — I don't mean in a bizarre way. She must live their dreams for them and remain a figure of mystery. Glamour is the most essential part of Hollywood."

Hollywood's first sex symbol then offered an appraisal of Hollywood's current sex symbol, Marilyn Monroe. "I think, like everyone else, that she is sexy. But I don't believe she likes it much, does she? She probably will have the same trouble I have had," Theda concluded prophetically. "She will never be able to live down her reputation."

As late as April 1954 Alan Brock was approaching Theda about working in summer stock. She was tempted, but wrote to him that "the only thing that would interest me would be the try-out of a new Broadway possibility."

But Theda's time was running out.

9 / The Unchastened Woman

By the spring of 1954, she hadn't been feeling quite right for some time. She'd been having more and more stomach upsets and digestive problems, and had been losing weight. Some rather unpleasant tests indicated even more unpleasant possibilities, and Theda's doctor, Newton Copp, suggested that she check into California Lutheran Hospital immediately.

She underwent surgery for colon cancer on June 30, 1954, but by then the cells had begun to spread. Theda, never a physically brave woman, underwent a total of four surgeries in 1954. It was too late: the cancer had taken over her liver. By early 1955 there was not enough healthy liver left to function properly and Theda failed quickly.

Theda re-entered California Lutheran Hospital for the last time on Valentine's Day 1955; she soon fell into a coma. She was given oxygen and intravenous fluid and nourishment, but there wasn't much more the doctors could do. Theda awoke briefly on April 5 and was able to take food, but she soon lost consciousness again. Lori and Charles had just left after a day-long visit when she died at 6:55 on the evening of April 7th, 1955. She was four months short of her seventieth birthday.

In her will, Theda left most of her $100,000 estate to Lori (who, by this time, was taking care of their quite elderly mother). She left her already wealthy husband $800 and her engagement and wedding rings "as a remembrance of our happy marriage." Another $1000 was left to Marque's widow Alma (Marque having died some years before). In 1957, Theda's extensive jewelry collection was exhibited at the Chicago Art Galleries and auctioned off for a considerable sum which went to her widower.

Theda's funeral service, on April 9, was a private family affair in Beverly Hills. She was cremated on the 11th and her ashes interred in Forest Lawn's Great Mausoleum — the same building that holds the remains of Jean Harlow, Marie Dressler, the Dolly sisters, Clark Gable and Carole Lombard.

The rest of her family didn't survive long. Pauline Bara died on the 4th of July, 1957, just five days before her 96th birthday. Charles Brabin died that autumn. He moved to Santa Monica after Theda's death and died there of a heart condition on November 3, 1957. He was seventy-five years old.

Lori also developed a heart condition. She became a patient at the newly opened and quite luxurious Marycrest Manor in Culver City, where the nuns still remember her as "a beautiful lady in every sense of the word." She died on August 4, 1965, at the age of sixty-eight.

By the time of Theda Bara's death in 1955, she was already a figure from the distant past. Her obituaries were lengthy and well-illustrated, but they spoke of her as a curiosity, an antique from another age. Nineteen-fifty-five was the year of Marilyn Monroe and James Dean — Theda looked somehow quaint and slightly ludicrous in her old photos. Silent movies had died as an art form twenty-five years previously; not old enough to be respected as history — just old enough to be considered funny and a little embarrassing.

Within ten years, film fans and historians began to take another look at Theda and search for her films. It was only then that it was discovered that Theda's films had died before Theda herself had.

Chapter 10

A Woman There Was

By the time Theda Bara died, silent films had become quaint camp, ripe for sledge-hammer subtle parody. In 1958, Marilyn Monroe posed as Theda in a half-joking, half-serious tribute. Lucille Ball imitated Theda more than once on TV. In 1960, comedy bandleader Spike Jones released an album called *Rides, Rapes and Rescues* which included the selection "Theda Barracuda meets Rudolph Vaselino." Badly edited "Fractured Flickers" with unbearable new subtitles and sound effects were shown on TV, giving a new generation a completely inaccurate view of silent films.

And, tragically, the real thing was vanishing from existence. Even during their heyday, no one really cared about silent films; few thought of them as a permanent art form. When talkies became popular, the old silents were like five-year-old newspapers: too old to be interesting; not old enough to be historical. At the few serious silent film revivals, the movies were usually projected at the wrong speed. Theda herself, seeing one of her old films in the talkie era, noted that she seemed to shoot through doors like a cannonball.

As early as 1935, film historians Theodore Huff and Mark Borgatta returned to Fort Lee to make *Ghost Town*, a heartbreaking documentary on the remains of the silent film studios. Only fifteen years after the industry had moved west, the old studios were crumbling ruins. Some had burned to their foundations, others left open to the elements. Behind the old Éclair studio, Huff and Borgatta found hundreds of abandoned film reels lying on the ground, ruined after years in the sun and rain. The Willat Studio, where Theda had shot many of her films, was nothing but a shell nearing collapse (today an apartment complex stands on the site).

A precious few people did care, and began collecting old films: James Card in the U. S., Henri Langlois in France, and British film critic Iris Barry, who in 1935 inaugurated the Film Library in New York's Museum of Modern Art. Barry began sweet-talking industry leaders, trying to get them to donate both money and old films to the collection. In 1936 she screened *A Fool There Was* at MoMA, which critic Sanderson Vanderbilt sniped "is fascinating only because [it's] funny."

But historians were horrified to discover what film makers already knew: by 1935 it was already too late; most of the flammable, quickly decomposing nitrate films had either vanished or were doomed. Throughout the silent era, films were recycled, melted down for their reusable silver content. Some were destroyed to keep other studios from pirating and re-showing them for profit. Many films were lost in fires; nitrate is extremely combustible and burns faster than dry leaves. Warehouse fires were a problem as early as 1914 when Lubin's vaults burned, destroying an entire city block.

On July 9, 1937, Fox's storage vault in Little Ferry, New Jersey exploded under the hot summer sun. Destroyed in the blast (along with much property and one life) were all of Fox's silent films. Every carefully labeled and preserved Theda Bara film went up in acrid smoke. The only remaining Bara films were in the hands of private collectors, fans, and stored away in a few old theaters. As the years passed, those copies disintegrated slowly but surely, and preservationists lacked the money, staff, and organizational abilities to track them down.

Even being sealed away in a museum archive was no guarantee of survival. The Museum of Modern Art lost Theda's *Cleopatra* and *Salome* in vault fires. Today, only two of her Fox films are known to exist: *A Fool There Was* and *East Lynne*. *The Unchas-*

tened Woman and a one-reel version of *Madame Mystery* also survive. Sadly, they represent four of her least impressive performances. Theda's own favorites, *Cleopatra*, *Under Two Flags* and *Kathleen Mavourneen*, are among her thirty-eight missing films.

Hundreds of film archives exist around the world, almost all of them understaffed and underfunded. They each possess thousands of reels of silent film, all of them slowly decaying and many of them unlabeled (American titles were often removed when sent to foreign countries). No one really knows how many silent films have been lost forever, but educated guesses run to seventy-five percent.

Lillian Gish spent the last few decades of her long life campaigning for film preservation. In 1988, she said, "we're the first people to leave a living history of our century, and we don't appreciate this . . . We're going to go down in disgrace 100, 200 years from now if that's not there for people to look at and learn from." When she died in 1993, Gish left $1.2 million to MoMA's film department.

Some films still turn up, as *East Lynne* did in 1971. In 1994, Australia's National Film Archive turned over more than 1600 silent films to the American Film Institute; many turned out to be one of a kind. In 1993, one reel of Garbo's only missing film, *The Divine Woman*, turned up in the basement of a Moscow archive, complete with Russian titles. There's a good chance that somewhere out there — unlabeled in a film vault, secreted away in a collector's attic, even under someone's front porch (it has happened), lies the last copy of a Theda Bara film.

If Theda's films have mostly vanished, her image has stayed firmly planted in the American consciousness. Since the 1960's,

Vamp: The Rise and Fall of Theda Bara

Logo from the Chicago International Film Festival. *Photo: Art Direction Magazine.*

Theda's face has been appearing regularly on greeting cards, advertisements, and posters. A still from *Salome* decorated the masthead of the 1960's counterculture newspaper *International Times* (the befuddled hippies apparently mistook her for "It" girl Clara Bow). That same still from *Salome* serves as the logo for the Chicago International Film Festival. Ads for everything from the Amsterdam Continental type foundry to Videotheque feature Theda's glaring visage. A statue of Theda in *Cleopatra* serves as a caryatid, holding up the ceiling of London's Museum of the Moving Image. Posters of Theda's shadowed eyes, black lips and outré poses have decorated the walls of a generation of college students. In 1995 Chanel launched a line of "Vamp" cosmetics.

In early 1992 a musical comedy called *Theda Bara and the Frontier Rabbi* opened after eight years in development. The show, by Bob Johnston and Jeff Hochhauser, got mixed reviews and played for about a year, but never made it past Off-Broadway. *Frontier Rabbi* told the story of the romance between Theda (played by Rachel Sweet and later by Jeanine LaManna) and social-reforming Rabbi Isaac Birnbaum. The play was respectful to Theda, although of course a great many liberties had to be taken for a good joke or

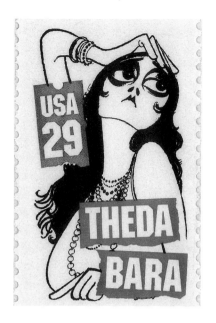

a song (among Theda's numbers were "There Are So Many Things That a Vampire Can't Do").

Theda was one of ten silent stars honored with U. S. Postal stamps in 1994. Caricatured by Al Hirschfeld (in a whimsical manner Theda probably would have detested), she joined Rudolph Valentino, Charlie Chaplin, Clara Bow and others on first-class letters that spring.

But even though Theda's image lives on, the loss of her film legacy has left her out in the cold. Every few years, a revival house may show *A Fool There Was*; but *East Lynne*, *The Unchastened Woman*, and *Madame Mystery* rarely see the light of day. Considering their quality, that may be just as well. But the missed opportunity to see her in action means that, compared with other stars of her era, Theda Bara is fading from history. Many film books brush her off as unimportant and faintly ludicrous, and the facts of her life still get confused with Fox's old press stories.

Vamp: The Rise and Fall of Theda Bara

A Theda Bara film festival would do more harm to her reputation than good, considering the quality of her surviving films. But perhaps Theda's luck will turn and more of her films will be discovered before they disintegrate. With the advent of video, her *Cleopatra, Salome,* and *Madame DuBarry* could find a huge audience.

The fate Theda envisioned for herself, however, is not likely to come about. In 1920 she told a reporter that her only films to have reached Australia were *The Two Orphans, Under Two Flags* and *Kathleen Mavourneen.* "They don't know me as a vampire there at all," she sighed wistfully.

Today, Theda is remembered — unjustly — as a vampire pure and simple. But unlike so many of her contemporaries, she *is* remembered, and will be long after all of her films have fallen to dust.

The End

Postscript

Presenting the most accurate information possible in the most readable way has been our overriding concern. We could have used an academic format and included every obligatory footnote, but that would have produced pages resembling shotgun targets. So we elected to eliminate the buckshot by not using footnotes in the text of this book. There would have been so many as to have been distracting to the reader, and so many of them would point to the collection of materials at Lincoln Center. Instead, the reader interested in further study is directed to the books and interviews noted in the bibliography and acknowledgements, and to the main source for information, Lincoln Center's Library for the Performing Arts in New York. Their collection of scrapbooks, photographs, loose clippings folders, magazines, and books proved invaluable not only for researching Theda, but also for researching films and theater of the period, and the lives and careers of her co-workers. My thanks to head librarian Robert Taylor and his tireless, patient staff (including the always efficient Edith Wiggins, whose wonderful vamp-like hairdos grew more inspiring with each passing day).

Three collections would prove most useful for those interested in further research. Two Robinson Locke scrapbooks on Theda Bara cover her life and career from 1914 through 1922. G. P. Sherwood scrapbook #MWEZ xxx nc 15,462 covers her life through the early 1940's.

Most interesting were Theda's two personal scrapbooks, the approximate size (and weight!) of marble tombstones. These contain reviews, interviews, and articles sent to her by her clipping service, fan mail, telegrams, Fox press releases, and other odds and ends (significantly, Theda saved her bad reviews as well as her good ones). Lori inherited them from Theda in 1955, and she in turn left them to Lincoln Center upon her death a decade later. Frustratingly, Theda's pre-1914 scrapbooks were destroyed in the fire described on page twenty-three of this book.

While the Robinson Locke and G. P. Sherwood collections are in relatively good condition, Theda's own scrapbooks are deteriorating rapidly. The clippings themselves are as fragile as autumn leaves, the bindings are largely gone, and the cheap cardboard backing is disintegrating. There is no way for Lincoln Center to preserve these books, as the clippings were haphazardly glued atop each other, each page holding up to five layers. These must be delicately lifted to be read and therefore cannot be photographed or transferred to microfilm.

Virtually all of the newspapers quoted come from the above sources. Where a newspaper's title is not noted, it was cut off or illegible in the scrapbook. About half of the magazine articles quoted are from Lincoln Center; the rest are from period magazines I bought or which were sent to me by film researchers and Theda Bara fans (Chester Clarke was particularly helpful here).

Much of the background material on Theda's childhood, Avondale in the 19th century, and the history of the Goodman family was unearthed by the very resourceful Kevin Grace. Film historians Kevin Brownlow and Robert Birchard helped to ensure that my facts were in order, while Karen Gershenhorn did an ace proofreading job (while anxiously awaiting the birth of her daughter Marisa). My editor, Grace Houghton, was delightfully patient and enthusiastic. And thanks as always to my mother, Eleanore Golden, for her role as Patroness of the Arts.

Filmography

Note: The date given is that of the earliest release; films took months to reach smaller towns and sometimes years before being released overseas. Sadly, the crew was rarely credited, so the names of many costume designers, camera people, art directors, and other deserving workers have been lost. The order of the cast listing — even character names — varies wildly from source to source.

THE STAIN
Pathé-Frères/Eclectic Film Company (July 1, 1914).
Director: Frank Powell. Scenario: Forrest Halsey, Robert H. Davis.
From a novel by Forrest Halsey and Robert H. Davis.
CAST: Edward José, Thurlow Bergen, Virginia Pearson, Eleanor Woodruff, Samuel Ryan, Theodosia deCoppett (as an extra).

A FOOL THERE WAS
William Fox Vaudeville Company (January 12, 1915).
Director/Scenario: Frank Powell. Scenario: Roy L. McCardell. Camera: Gene Santoreilli and George Schneiderman. Adapted from the play by Porter Emerson Browne. 6 reels (about 70 minutes). Re-released June 1918 at 5 reels.
A sex-crazed fiend destroys an American diplomat.
CAST: Theda Bara (The Vampire); Edward José (John Schuyler); May Allison (the wife's sister); Clifford Bruce (Tom); Mabel Fremyear (Kate Schuyler); Victor Benoit (Parmalee); Runa Hodges (Schuyler's daughter); Minna Gale (the doctor's fiancée); Frank Powell (the doctor); Creighton Hale.

Vamp: The Rise and Fall of Theda Bara

THE KREUTZER SONATA
Fox Film Corporation (March 1, 1915).
Director/Scenario: Herbert Brenon. Camera: Philip E. Rosen. Adapted from plays by Leo Tolstoy and Jacob Gordin. 5 reels (about 60 minutes).
A woman steals her Orthodox Jewish sister's husband, with fatal results for all.
CAST: Nance O'Neil (Miriam Friedlander); Theda Bara (Celia Friedlander); William E. Shay (Gregor Randar); Mimi Yvonne.

THE CLEMENCEAU CASE
Fox Film Corporation (April 19, 1915).
Director/Scenario: Herbert Brenon. Camera: Philip E. Rosen. Adapted from the novel by Alexandre Dumas. 6 reels (about 70 minutes). Re-released July 1918.
An artist's model aims to destroy her husband's best friend.
CAST: Theda Bara (Iza); William E. Shay (Pierre Clemenceau); Mrs. Allan Walker (Marie, his mother); Stuart Holmes (Constantin Ritz); Jane Lee (Janet); Mrs. Cecil Raleigh (Countess Dobronowska); Frank Goldsmith (Duke Sergius); Sidney Shields (Madame Ritz).

THE DEVIL'S DAUGHTER
Fox Film Corporation (June 16, 1915).
Director: Frank Powell. Ass't. Director: George I. Barber. Scenario: Garfield Thompson. Camera: David Calcagni, Caesar Ponci, Arthur Boeger. Adapted from an unpublished play by Joseph H. Trant, based on the novel *La Gioconda*, by Gabriele D'Annunzio.
An artist's model wreaks vengeance on the male sex for their wrongs, then goes mad.
CAST: Theda Bara (La Gioconda); Paul Doucet (Lucio Settala); Victor Benoit (Cosimo Daldo); Robert Wayne (Lorenzo Gaddi); Jane Lee (Little Beata); Doris Haywood (Silvia Settala); Jane Miller (Francesca Doni); Elaine Evans (La Sirenetta); Edouard Durad (Roffiano); Clifford Bruce.

LADY AUDLEY'S SECRET
Fox Film Corporation (August 4, 1915).
Director: Marshall Farnum. Scenario: Mary Asquith. Camera: Norton "Doc" Davis. Adapted from the 1862 novel by M. E. Braddon. 5 reels (about 60 minutes).
From a popular Victorian novel and play about a respectable wife with a dark secret.
CAST: Theda Bara (Helen Talboys); Clifford Bruce; William Riley Hatch (Luke Martin); Stephen Gratten; Warner Richmond.

THE TWO ORPHANS
Fox Film Corporation (September 5, 1915)
Director/Scenario: Herbert Brenon. Camera: Philip E. Rosen. Adapted from the 1875 play by Adolphe D'Ennery and Eugene Corman. 7 reels (about 85 minutes). Re-released 1918.
Foundling and her blind sister endure poverty and kidnapping before finding their happy ending.
CAST: Theda Bara (Henriette); Jean Sothern (Louise); William E. Shay (Chevalier de Vaudrey); Herbert Brenon (Pierre); Gertrude Berkley (Mother Frochard); Frank Goldsmith (Marquis de Presles); E. L. Fernandez (Jacques); Sheridan Block (Count De Liniere); Mrs. Cecil Raleigh (Countess De Liniere); John Daley Murphy (Picard).

SIN
Fox Film Corporation (October 3, 1915).
Director/Scenario: Herbert Brenon. Camera: Philip E. Rosen. Based on "Jewels of the Madonna," an unpublished story by Herbert Brenon. 5 reels (about 60 minutes).
An Italian peasant girl turns vamp when wronged by a New York Mafioso.
CAST: Theda Bara (Rosa); William E. Shay (Luigi); Warner Oland (Pietro); Mrs. Louise Rial; Henry Leone.

CARMEN
Fox Film Corporation (November 1, 1915).
Director/Scenario: Raoul A. Walsh. Ass't. Director: M. H. Morange. Camera: Georges Benoit, George Schneiderman. Technical Director: Edward Velasquez. Adapted from the 1845 novel by Prosper Merimée. 5 reels (about 60 minutes).
Fiery cigarette factory girl wreaks havoc among the men of Spain.
CAST: Theda Bara (Carmen); Einar Linden (Don José); Carl Harbaugh (Escamillo); James A. Marcus (Dancaire); Elsie McCloud (Michaela); Fay Tunis (Carlotta); Emil de Varney (Captain Morales); Joseph P. Green.

THE GALLEY SLAVE
Fox Film Corporation (November 28, 1915).
Director: J. Gordon Edwards. Scenario: Clara S. Beranger. Adapted from the 1879 play by Bartley Campbell.
A wronged wife seeks vengeance on her wicked husband.
CAST: Theda Bara (Francesca Brabaut); Stuart Holmes (Antoine Brabaut); Claire Whitney (Cecily Blaine); Lillian Lawrence (Mrs. Blaine); Jane Lee (Dolores); Ben Hendricks (Mr. Blaine); Hardee Kirklin (Baron La Bois); Henry Leone; A. H. Van Buren.

DESTRUCTION
Fox Film Corporation (December 26, 1915).
Director/Scenario: Will S. Davis. Story: Bernard Chapin.
A foundry owner's wife stirs up labor trouble and family jealousies.
CAST: Theda Bara (Ferdinande Martin); Joseph Furney (John Froment, Sr.); Carlton Macey (John Froment, Jr.); Esther H. Hoier (Josine Walker); Warner Oland (Delaveau); J. Herbert Frank (Dave Walker); Frank Evans (Bonner); Arthur Morrison (Lang); Gaston Bell (John Froment, III); Master Tansey (Jimmie); J. Walker.

THE SERPENT
Fox Film Corporation (January 23, 1916).
Director/Scenario: Raoul A. Walsh. Cameraman: Georges Benoit.
Adapted from "The Wolf's Claw," an unpublished story by Philip
Bartholmae. 6 reels (about 70 minutes). Re-released January 1919.
A Russian peasant girl turns vamp when wronged by a Grand
Duke; it all turns out to be a bad dream.
CAST: Theda Bara (Vania Lazar); George Walsh (Andrei Sobi);
James Marcus (Ivan Lazar); Lillian Hathaway (Martza Lazar);
Charles Craig (Grand Duke Valonoff); Carl Harbaugh (Prince Valonoff);
Nan Carter (Erna Lachno); Marcel Morhange (Gregoire); Ben Nedell.

GOLD AND THE WOMAN
Fox Film Corporation (March 12, 1916).
Director: James Vincent. Scenario: Mary Murillo, based on her
unpublished story "Retribution." 6 reels (about 70 minutes).
A Mexican vamp destroys an equally evil English army man whose
ancestor had cheated Indians out of their land.
CAST: Theda Bara (Juliet De Cordova); H. Cooper Cliffe (Col.
Dent); Alma Hanlon (Hester Grey); Harry Hilliard (Leo Duskara);
Chief Black Eagle (Leelo Duskara); Jude Hurley (Duskara's
squaw); Caroline Harris; Ted Griffin; Louis Stern; James Sheehan;
Carlton Macey; Frank Whitson; Pauline Barry; Carter B. Harkness.

THE ETERNAL SAPHO
Fox Film Corporation (May 7, 1916).
Director: Bertram Bracken. Scenario: Mary Murillo. Camera: Rial
Schellinger. Adapted from the novel "Sappho," by Daudet. 5 reels
(about 60 minutes).
Rise and fall of a Greenwich Village artist's model.
CAST: Theda Bara (Laura Gubbins); Warner Oland (H. Coudal);
Frank Norcross (Mr. Gubbins); George MacQuarrie (Jack McCul-
lough); Walter Lewis (Mr. Malvern); Hattie Delano (Mrs. Malvern);

Laura Gubbins gets the once-over from a pack of Bohemian artists in *The Eternal Sapho* (1916). The mustachioed gentleman at the left is Warner Oland. *Photo: Wisconsin Center for Film and Theater Research.*

James Cooley (Billy Malvern); Einar Linden (John Drummond); Mary Martin (Mrs. Drummond); Kittens Reichert (Peggy); Carolyn Harris (Mother Gubbins).

EAST LYNNE
Fox Film Corporation (June 18, 1916).
Director: Bertram Bracken. Scenario: Mary Murillo. Camera: Rial Schellinger. Adapted from the 1861 novel by Mrs. Henry Wood. 5 reels (about 60 minutes).
Another Victorian novel and play about a divorcée who comes to a bad end.
CAST: Theda Bara (Lady Isabel); Claire Whitney (Barbara Hare); Stuart Holmes (Captain Levison); William H. Tooker (Judge Hare); Stanhope Wheatcroft (Richard Hare), Ben Deely (Archibald Carlisle); Eugenie Woodward (Mrs. Hare); H. F. Hoffman (Otway

Bethel); James O'Connor (Old Hellijohn); Emma Fitzroy (Cornelia); Loel Stewart (Little Isabel); Elden Stewart (Little Willie); Frank Norcross; Ethel Fleming; H. Evans, Velma Whitman.

UNDER TWO FLAGS
Fox Film Corporation (July 31, 1916).
Director: J. Gordon Edwards. Scenario: George Hall. Camera: Philip E. Rosen. Adapted from the 1867 novel by Ouida (Louise de la Ramee). 6 reels (about 70 minutes). Re-released January 1919.
Love comes with tragic results to the heroic adventuress of the French Foreign Legion.
CAST: Theda Bara (Cigarette); Herbert Heyes (Bertie Cecil); Stuart Holmes (Chateauroye); Stanhope Wheatcroft (Berkeley Cecil); Joseph Crehan (Rake); Charles Craig (Rockingham); Claire Whitney (Venetia).

HER DOUBLE LIFE
Fox Film Corporation (September 10, 1916).
Director: J. Gordon Edwards. Scenario: Mary Murillo, based on her unpublished story, "The New Magdelen." Camera: Philip E. Rosen. 6 reels (about 70 minutes).
A poor but good-hearted Cockney girl masquerades as a noble-woman.
CAST: Theda Bara (Mary Doone); Stuart Holmes (Lloyd Stanley); A. H. Van Buren (Elliott Clifford); Walter Law (longshoreman); Madeleine Le Nard (Ethel Wardley); Carey Lee (longshoreman's wife); Katherine Lee (young Mary); Lucia Moore (Lady Clifford); Franklin Hanna (doctor); Jane Lee (naughty girl).

ROMEO AND JULIET
Fox Film Corporation (October 22, 1916).
Director: J. Gordon Edwards. Scenario: Adrian Johnson. Adapted from the play by William Shakespeare. 7 reels (about 85 minutes).
A fairly straightforward version of Shakespeare's play.

CAST: Theda Bara (Juliet); Harry Hilliard (Romeo); Glen White (Mercutio); Walter Law (Friar Lawrence); John Webb Dillon (Tybalt); Einar Linden (Paris); Edwin Eaton (Montague); Edwin Holt (Capulet); Alice Gale (Nurse); Victory Bateman (Lady Montague); Helen Tracy (Lady Capulet); Jane and Katherine Lee.

THE VIXEN
Fox Film Corporation (December 3, 1916).
Director: J. Gordon Edwards. Scenario: Mary Murillo. Camera: Philip E. Rosen.
Woman tries to break up her sister's marriage.
CAST: Theda Bara (Elsie Drummond); Mary Martin (Helen Drummond); A. H. Van Buren (Martin Stevens); Herbert Heyes (Knowles Murray); George Clarke (Admiral Drummond); Carl Gerard (Charlie Drummond); George Odell (butler); Jane and Katherine Lee.

THE DARLING OF PARIS
Fox Film Corporation (January 22, 1917).
Director: J. Gordon Edwards. Scenario: Adrian Johnson. Camera: Philip E. Rosen. Adapted from the 1831 novel "Notre Dame de Paris" by Victor Hugo. 6 reels (about 70 minutes). Re-released February 1919.
A very loose adaptation of Hugo's tale.
CAST: Theda Bara (Esmeralda); Glen White (Quasimodo); Walter Law (Claude Frallo); Herbert Heyes (Captain Phoebus); Carey Lee (Paquette); Alice Gale (Gypsy Queen); John Webb Dillon (Clopin); Louis Dean (Gringoulier).

THE TIGER WOMAN
Fox Film Corporation (February 18, 1917).
Director: J. Gordon Edwards. Scenario: Adrian Johnson. Camera: Philip E. Rosen. Scenario: Adrian Johnson, based on his unpublished story, "Quicksands." 6 reels (about 70 minutes).

A Russian villainess' road to ruin via murder and theft.
CAST: Theda Bara (Princess Petrovitch); E. F. Rogerman (Prince Petrovitch); Glen White (Edwin Harris); Mary Martin (Mrs. Mark Harris); John Webb Dillon (Stefan); Louis Dean (Baron Kesingi); Emil De Varney (Count Verstorf); Herbert Heyes (Mark Harris); Edwin Holt (Mr. Harris); Florence Martin (Marion Harding); Kate Blanke (Marion's mother); George Clarke (Marion's father); Kittens Reichert (the Harris' child).

HER GREATEST LOVE
Fox Film Corporation (April 2, 1917).
Director: J. Gordon Edwards. Scenario: Adrian Johnson. Camera: Philip E. Rosen. Adapted from the 1880 novel "Moths" by Ouida. 5 reels (about 60 minutes).
A good girl wronged by her wicked family.
CAST: Theda Bara (Vera Herbert); Glen White (Lord Jura); Harry Hilliard (Lucien Correze); Walter Law (Prince Zouroff); Marie Curtis (Lady Dolly); Alice Gale (Nurse); Callie Torres (Jeanne De Sonnaz).

HEART AND SOUL
Fox Film Corporation (May 21, 1917).
Director: J. Gordon Edwards. Scenario: Adrian Johnson. Camera: Philip E. Rosen. Adapted from the 1887 novel "Jess" by Rider Haggard.
A Hawaiian maiden sacrifices herself for her sister's happiness.
CAST: Theda Bara (Jess); Harry Hilliard (John Neihl); Glen White (Jantze); Claire Whitney (Bess); Walter Law (Martin Brummond); Edwin Holt (Silas Croft); John Webb Dillon (Pedro); Alice Gale (Dulce); Kittens Reichert (Bess, in prologue); Margaret Laird (Jess, in prologue).

CAMILLE

Fox Film Corporation (September 30, 1917).

Director: J. Gordon Edwards. Scenario: Adrian Johnson. Camera: Rial Schellinger. Adapted from the 1848 novel and 1852 play "La Dame aux Camellias" by Alexandre Dumas. 5 reels (about 60 minutes). A modern-dress re-telling of the doomed French courtesan's life.

CAST: Theda Bara (Marguerite Gautier); Albert Roscoe (Armand Duvall); Walter Law (de Varville); Glen White (Gaston Rieux); Alice Gale (Madame Prudence); Claire Whitney (Celeste).

CLEOPATRA

Fox Film Corporation (October 14, 1917).

Director: J. Gordon Edwards. Scenario: Adrian Johnson. Camera: Rial Schellinger, John W. Boyle, George Schneiderman. Editor: Edward McDermott. Scenario: Adrian Johnson, based on his original story adapted from the play by Sardou. 11 reels (about 130 minutes). The life and loves of Egypt's last queen.

CAST: Theda Bara (Cleopatra); Fritz Leiber (Caesar); Thurston Hall (Marc Antony); Albert Roscoe (Pharon); Genevieve Blinn (Octavia); Henri de Vries (Octavius); Dorothy Drake (Charmain); Dell Duncan (Iris); Hector V. Sarno (Messenger); Herschel Mayall; Art Acord (Kephren).

WILLIAM FOX PRESENTS
THEDA BARA IN THE **ROSE OF BLOOD**
By RICHARD ORDYNSKI   Staged by J. GORDON EDWARDS
STANDARD PICTURES

Poster art from *The Rose of Blood* (1917). *Photo: Jerry Ohlinger.*

THE ROSE OF BLOOD
Fox Film Corporation (November 4, 1917).
Director: J. Gordon Edwards. Scenario: Bernard McConville.
Camera: Rial Schellinger, John W. Boyle. Adapted from "The Red
Rose," an unpublished story by Richard Ordynski.
A Russian woman fights on the side of the Revolutionaries against
the Tsardom.
CAST: Theda Bara (Lisza Tapenka); Richard Ordynski (Vassya);
Charles Clary (Prince Arbassoff); Herschel Mayall (Kaliensky);
Marie Keirnan (Kostya); Bert Turner (Princess Arbassoff);
Genevieve Blinn (Governess); Joe King (Prime Minister); Hector V.
Sarno (revolutionist).

Left: On location for *Cleopatra* (1917). *Photo: Robert S. Birchard.*

MADAME DU BARRY

Fox Film Corporation (December 30, 1917).

Director: J. Gordon Edwards. Scenario: Adrian Johnson. Costumes: George Hopkins. Camera: Rial Schellinger, John W. Boyle. Adapted from a novel by Alexandre Dumas. 7 reels (about 85 minutes).

The life and death of Louis XV's mistress.

CAST: Theda Bara (Madame Du Barry); Charles Clary (Louis XV); Herschel Mayall (Jean Du Barry); Fred Church (Conte Brissac); Genevieve Blinn (Duchesse de Gaoumont); Willard Louis (Guillaume De Barry); Hector Sarno (Lebel); Dorothy Drake (Henriette); Rosita Marstini (Mother Savord); Joe King; James Conley; A. Fremont.

THE FORBIDDEN PATH

Fox Film Corporation (February 3, 1918).

Director: J. Gordon Edwards. Scenario: E. Lloyd Sheldon, Adrian Johnson. Costumes: George Hopkins. Camera: John W. Boyle. Scenario: E. Lloyd Sheldon and Adrian Johnson, based on "From the Depths," an unpublished story by E. Lloyd Sheldon. 6 reels (about 70 minutes).

An innocent girl turned dissipated vamp by a Greenwich Village artist.

CAST: Theda Bara (Mary Lynde); Hugh Thompson (Robert Sinclair); Sidney Mason (Felix Benavente); Walter Law (Mr. Lynde); Florence Martin (Barbara Reynolds); Wynne Hope Allen (Mrs. Lynde); Alphonse Ethier (William Sinclair); Lisle Leigh (Mrs. Byrne); Reba Porter (Tessie Byrne).

THE SOUL OF BUDDHA

Fox Film Corporation (April 21, 1918).

Director: J. Gordon Edwards. Scenario: Adrian Johnson. Costumes: George Hopkins. Camera: John W. Boyle. 5 reels (about 60 minutes).

An unwilling Javanese Priestess destroys a Scottish visitor.

CAST: Theda Bara (Bavahari); Hugh Thompson (Sir John Dare); Victor Kennard (Ysora, a priest); Anthony Merlow (M. Romaine);

As a wayward artist's model in *The Forbidden Path* (1918). *Photo: Archive Photos.*

Florence Martin (his wife); Jack Ridgway (her father); Henry Warwick (stage manager).

UNDER THE YOKE
Fox Film Corporation (June 9, 1918)
Director: J. Gordon Edwards. Scenario: Adrian Johnson. Costumes: George Hopkins. Camera: John W. Boyle, Harry Gerstad. Scenario: Adrian Johnson, adapted from "Maria of the Roses," an unpublished story by George Scarborough.
Romance flares during Philippine Revolution.
CAST: Theda Bara (Maria Valverde); Albert Roscoe (Captain Paul Winter); G. Raymond Nye (Diabolo Ramirez); E. B. Tilton (Don Ramon Valverde); Carrie Clark Ward (Duenna).

Portrait still from *Salome* (1918). *Photo: Jerry Ohlinger.*

SALOME

Fox Film Corporation (August 10, 1918).

Director: J. Gordon Edwards. Scenario: Adrian Johnson. Costumes: George Hopkins. Camera: George Schneiderman, John W. Boyle, Harry Gerstad. 8 reels (about 100 minutes).

The life and death of the Biblical princess, with help from Oscar Wilde.

CAST: Theda Bara (Salome); G. Raymond Nye (Herod); Albert Roscoe (John the Baptist); Bertram Grassby (Aristobulus); Herbert Heyes (Schemus); Genevieve Blinn (Herodius); Vera Doria (Naomi); Alfred Fremont (Gadeus).

WHEN A WOMAN SINS
Fox Film Corporation (September 28, 1918).
Director: J. Gordon Edwards. Costumes: George Hopkins. Scenario: E. Lloyd Sheldon. Camera: John W. Boyle. Adapted from the story "The Message of the Lilies" by Betta Breuil. 7 reels (about 85 minutes).
A foolish but good-hearted girl falls in love with the son of a man she accidentally killed.
CAST: Theda Bara (Lillian Marchard/Poppea); Albert Roscoe (Michael West); Joseph Swickard (Mortimer West); Ogden Crane (Dr. Stone); Alfred Fremont (Augustus Van Brooks); Jack Rollens (Reggie West); Genevieve Blinn (Mrs. West).

THE SHE-DEVIL
Fox Film Corporation (November 10, 1918)
Director/Scenario: J. Gordon Edwards. Costumes/Story: George Hopkins. Camera: John W. Boyle, Harry Gerstad. 6 reels (about 70 minutes).
A Spanish dancer cavorts with bandits and artists.
CAST: Theda Bara (Lolette); Albert Roscoe (Maurice Tabor); Frederick Bond (Apollo); George A. McDaniel (The Tiger).

THE LIGHT
Fox Film Corporation (January 12, 1919).
Director: J. Gordon Edwards. Costumes: George Hopkins. Scenario: Adrian Johnson and Charles Kenyon, adapted from an unpublished story by Luther Reed and Brett Page. 5 reels (about 60 minutes).
A female gangster becomes a nurse.
CAST: Theda Bara (Blanche DuMond); Eugene Ormande (Chabin); Robert Walker (Etienne Deschette); George Revenant (Auchat); Florence Martin (Jeanette).

WHEN MEN DESIRE

Fox Film Corporation (March 9, 1919).

Director: J. Gordon Edwards. Scenario: Adrian Johnson. Costumes: George Hopkins. Camera: John W. Boyle. Adapted from the story "The Scarlet Altars" by E. Lloyd Sheldon and J. Searle Dawley. 5 reels (about 60 minutes).

A brave American girl in Germany is caught behind the lines when WWI breaks out.

CAST: Theda Bara (Marie Lohr); Fleming Ward (Robert Stedman); G. Raymond Nye (Major Wolf Von Rohn); Florence Martin (Elsie Henner); Maude Hill (Lola Santez); Edward Elkas (Professor Lohr).

THE SIREN'S SONG

Fox Film Corporation (May 4, 1919)

Director: J. Gordon Edwards. Scenario: Charles Kenyon, based on his unpublished story. Costumes: George Hopkins. Camera: John W. Boyle. 5 reels (about 60 minutes).

A lighthouse keeper's daughter becomes a famous singer.

CAST: Theda Bara (Marie Bernais); Alfred Fremont (Jules Bernais); Ruth Handworth (Aunt Caroline); L. C. Shumway (Raoul Nieppe); Albert Roscoe (Gaspard Prevost); Paul Weigel (Hector Remey); Carrie Clark Ward (Paulette Remey).

A WOMAN THERE WAS

Fox Film Corporation (June 1, 1919).

Director: J. Gordon Edwards. Scenario: Adrian Johnson. Costumes: George Hopkins. Camera: John W. Boyle. Adapted from the story "Creation's Tears" by George Hopkins. 5 reels (about 60 minutes).

A South Seas island girl falls in love with a missionary.

CAST: Theda Bara (Princess Zara); William B. Davidson (Winthrop Stark); Robert Elliott (Pulke); Claude Payton (High Priest); John Ardizoni (King).

KATHLEEN MAVOURNEEN
Fox Film Corporation (August 19, 1919).
Director/Scenario: Charles J. Brabin. Costumes: George Hopkins.
Insert and title photography: Richard Maedler. Adapted from the
play by Dion Boucicault, the poem by Tom Moore, and the song by
Annie Crawford. 6 reels (about 70 minutes).
Irish girl in love with good boy is pursued by wicked landowner.
CAST: Theda Bara (Kathleen); Edward O'Connor (Kathleen's
father); Jennie Dickenson (Kathleen's mother); Raymond McKee
(Terrence O'Moore); Marc McDermott (The Squire of Tralee);
Marcia Harris (Lady Clancarthy); Henry Hallam (Sir John Clan-
carthy); Harry Gripp (Denis O'Rourke); Morgan Thorpe (Father
O'Flynn).

LA BELLE RUSSE
Fox Film Corporation (September 21, 1919).
Director/Scenario: Charles J. Brabin. Costumes: George Hopkins.
Camera: George Lane. Adapted from the 1882 play by David
Belasco. 6 reels (about 70 minutes).
Twin sisters — one good and one bad — clash.
CAST: Theda Bara (La Belle Russe/Fleurette); Warburton Gamble
(Phillip Sackton); Marian Stewart (Phillip Sackton, Jr.); Robert Lee
Keeling (Sir James Sackton); William B. Davidson (Brand); Alice
Wilson (Lady Sackton); Robert Vivian (butler); Lewis Broughton.

THE LURE OF AMBITION
Fox Film Corporation (November 16, 1919).
Director/Scenario: Edmund Lawrence. Costumes: George Hop-
kins. Camera: H. Alderson Leach. Insert and title photography:
Richard Maedler. Adapted from an unpublished story by Julia
Burnham.
A poor spurned girl gets revenge on British society and marries a
Duke.
CAST: Theda Bara (Olga Dolan); Thurlow Bergen (Duke of Rut-

ledge); William B. Davidson (Hon. Cyril Ralston); Dan Mason (Sylvester Dolan); Ida Waterman (Duchess); Amelia Gardner (Lady Constance); Robert Paton Gibbs (Miguel Lopez); Dorothy Drake (Muriel Ralston); Peggy Parr (Minnie Dolan); Tammany Young (Dan Hicks).

THE UNCHASTENED WOMAN
Chadwick Pictures Corporation (November 16, 1925).
Director: James Young. Scenario: Douglas Z. Doty. Camera: William O'Connell. Art Directors: Clifford P. Saum, Earl Sibley. Editor: Sam Zimbalist. Adapted from the 1915 play by Louise K. Anspacher. 7 reels (about 85 minutes).
Woman turns vamp when she finds her husband is two-timing her. CAST: Theda Bara (Caroline Knollys); Wyndham Standing (Hubert Knollys); Dale Fuller (Hildegarde Sanbury); John Miljan (Lawrence Sanbury); Eileen Percy (Emily Maddon); Dot Farley; Harry Northrup (Michael Krellin); Mayme Kelso (Susan Ambie); Kate Price; Eric Mayne; Frederic Kovert.

MADAME MYSTERY
Pathé/Hal Roach Studios (March 12, 1926)
Directors: Richard Wallace and Stan Laurel. Ass't. Director: Jean
Yarbrough. Scenario: Hal Roach. Camera: Floyd Jackman. Cos-
tumes: Will Lambert. Properties: Morey Lightfoot. Cutter: R. L.
Muesler. Tutor: Elva Helson. 2 reels (about 20 minutes).
French spy smuggles bomb aboard ship.
CAST: Theda Bara; James Finlayson; Tyler Brooke; Oliver Hardy;
Fred Malatesta, Sam Brooks, R. E. Madeson, Martha Sleeper.

Left: Eileen Percy and Theda Bara in *The Unchastened Woman* (1925). *Photo:*
Robert S. Birchard.

Cleopatra (1917). *Photos: Robert S. Birchard.*

Bibliography

Altomara, Rita Ecke. *Hollywood on the Palisades*. New York: Garland Publishing, 1983.

Bartelt, Chuck and Bergeron, Barbara (editors). *Variety Obituaries.* New York: Garland Publishing, 1989.

Blum, Daniel. *Great Stars of the American Stage*. New York: Greenberg: Publisher, 1952.

_____. *A Pictorial History of the Silent Screen*. New York: Grosset & Dunlap Publishers, 1953.

_____. *A Pictorial History of the American Theatre*. New York: Crown Publishers, 1977.

Bodeen, DeWitt. "Theda Bara." *Films in Review*, May 1968 (pages 266-287).

Bowser, Eileen. *The Transformation of Cinema, 1907—1915*. New York: Macmillan, 1990.

Brownlow, Kevin, & Gill, David. *Hollywood*. London: Photoplay Productions, 1979 (television documentary).

Card, James. *Seductive Cinema*. New York: Alfred A. Knopf, 1994.

Cooper, Miriam. *Dark Lady of the Silents*. New York: Bobbs-Merrill, 1973.

Drew, William M. *Speaking of Silents*. Vestal, NY: The Vestal Press, Ltd., 1989.

Engstead, John. *Star Shots*. New York: E. P. Dutton, 1978.

Fountain, Leatrice Gilbert. *Dark Star*. New York: St. Martin's Press, 1985.

Gish, Lillian: *The Movies, Mr. Griffith and Me* (with Ann Pinchot). Englewood Cliffs, NJ: Prentice-Hall, Inc., 1969.

————. *Dorothy and Lillian Gish*. New York: Charles Scribner's Sons, 1973.

Goldman, Herbert G. *Fanny Brice, The Original Funny Girl*. New York: Oxford University Press, 1992.

Hampton, Benjamin B. *A History of the Movies*. New York: Covici Friede Publishers, 1931.

Hayne, Donald (editor). *The Autobiography of Cecil B. DeMille*. Englewood Cliffs, NJ: Prentice Hall, Inc., 1959.

Henig, Robin Marantz. *A Dancing Matrix: Voyages Along the Viral Frontier*. New York: Alfred A. Knopf, 1992.

Keylin, Arleen. *Hollywood Album*. New York: Arno Press, 1977.

————. *Hollywood Album 2*. New York: Arno Press, 1979.

Koszarski, Richard. *An Evening's Entertainment: The Age of the Silent Feature Picture, 1915–1928*. New York: Macmillan, 1990.

Lamparski, Richard. *Whatever Became Of . . . ?* (volumes 1—11). New York: Crown Publishers, Inc., 1967—1989.

Leyda, Jay. *Voices of Film Experience*. New York: Macmillan, 1977.

Mordden, Ethan. *Movie Star: A Look at the Women Who Made Hollywood*. New York: St. Martin's Press, 1983.

Musser, Charles. *The Emergence of Cinema: The American Screen to 1907*. New York: Macmillan, 1990.

Negri, Pola. *Memoirs of a Star*. New York: Doubleday & Company, 1970.

Nuland, Sherwin B. *How We Die*. New York: Alfred A. Knopf, 1994.

Parish, James Robert. *The Fox Girls*. New Rochelle, NY: Arlington House, 1971.

Pogle, Frances Putnam. *The Standard American Speaker and Entertainer*. Philadelphia: Standard Publishing, 1901.

Pratt, George. *Spellbound in Darkness: A History of the Silent Film*. Greenwich, CT: New York Graphic Society, 1973.

Ramsey, Terry. *A Million and One Nights*. New York: Simon & Schuster, Inc., 1926.

Rawlence, Christopher. *The Missing Reel*. New York: Atheneum, 1990.

Sinclair, Upton. *Upton Sinclair Presents William Fox*. Los Angeles: Upton Sinclair, 1933.

Sleeper, Jim. *Great Movies Shot in Orange County*. Trabuco Canyon, CA: California Classics, 1980.

Slide, Anthony. *Early American Cinema*. New York: A. S. Barnes & Company, 1970.

_____. *Early Women Directors*. New York: A. S. Barnes & Company, 1977.

_____. *Silent Portraits*. Vestal, NY: The Vestal Press, Ltd., 1989.

_____. *Nitrate Won't Wait*. Jefferson, NC: McFarland & Co., Inc., 1992.

Wagenknecht, Edward. *The Movies in the Age of Innocence*. New York: Ballantine Books, 1962.

Walker, Alexander. *The Celluloid Sacrifice*. Baltimore: Penguin Books, 1968.

Zierold, Norman. *Sex Goddesses of the Silent Screen*. Chicago: Henry Regnerey Company, 1973.

Index

Page numbers in italics refer to illustrations. Listings in italics refer to titles of films, plays, songs, books, or television shows. Neither Theda Bara herself nor her longtime studio, Fox Film Corporation, are listed herein, as they are mentioned throughout the text.

About the Author

EVE GOLDEN, whose teachers used to tell her, "you'll never get anywhere by watching old movies and being sarcastic," now earns her living by watching old movies and being sarcastic. Born and raised on Philadelphia's Main Line, she works in New York as a contributing editor and columnist for *Movieline* and writes for *Classic Images, Men's Health, AMC, Playboy,* and *A & E Monthly,* among others. Her previous book, *Platinum Girl: The Life and Legends of Jean Harlow,* was published by Abbeville Press in 1991.